CAMBRIDGE LIBRARY COLLECTION

Books of enduring scholarly value

Religion

For centuries, scripture and theology were the focus of prodigious amounts of scholarship and publishing, dominated in the English-speaking world by the work of Protestant Christians. Enlightenment philosophy and science, anthropology, ethnology and the colonial experience all brought new perspectives, lively debates and heated controversies to the study of religion and its role in the world, many of which continue to this day. This series explores the editing and interpretation of religious texts, the history of religious ideas and institutions, and not least the encounter between religion and science.

The Religions of the World and Their Relations to Christianity

The Religions of the World and Their Relations to Christianity (1847) derives from a series of eight lectures by the renowned theologian and political radical F. D. Maurice (1805–1872). They were given in a series established by Robert Boyle in 1691 as a stipulation of his will and intended 'for proving the Christian Religion against notorious Infidels.' Maurice both abides by and transforms this charge, examining 'the great Religious Systems ... not going into their details ... but enquiring what was their main characteristical principle.' In this important early work of comparative religious scholarship, Maurice investigates the theological foundations of the major world religions — Christianity, Islam, Hinduism, Buddhism and Judaism — as well as what he calls the 'defunct' faiths of ancient Greek, Rome, Egypt, Persia and Scandinavia. The resulting text is a rich work of theological enquiry and a valuable testament to a central nineteenth-century religious thinker.

T0381853

Cambridge University Press has long been a pioneer in the reissuing of out-of-print titles from its own backlist, producing digital reprints of books that are still sought after by scholars and students but could not be reprinted economically using traditional technology. The Cambridge Library Collection extends this activity to a wider range of books which are still of importance to researchers and professionals, either for the source material they contain, or as landmarks in the history of their academic discipline.

Drawing from the world-renowned collections in the Cambridge University Library, and guided by the advice of experts in each subject area, Cambridge University Press is using state-of-the-art scanning machines in its own Printing House to capture the content of each book selected for inclusion. The files are processed to give a consistently clear, crisp image, and the books finished to the high quality standard for which the Press is recognised around the world. The latest print-on-demand technology ensures that the books will remain available indefinitely, and that orders for single or multiple copies can quickly be supplied.

The Cambridge Library Collection will bring back to life books of enduring scholarly value (including out-of-copyright works originally issued by other publishers) across a wide range of disciplines in the humanities and social sciences and in science and technology.

The Religions of the World and Their Relations to Christianity

FREDERICK DENISON MAURICE

CAMBRIDGE UNIVERSITY PRESS

Cambridge, New York, Melbourne, Madrid, Cape Town, Singapore,
São Paolo, Delhi, Dubai, Tokyo

Published in the United States of America by Cambridge University Press, New York

www.cambridge.org
Information on this title: www.cambridge.org/9781108007931

© in this compilation Cambridge University Press 2009

This edition first published 1847
This digitally printed version 2009

ISBN 978-1-108-00793-1 Paperback

This book reproduces the text of the original edition. The content and language reflect
the beliefs, practices and terminology of their time, and have not been updated.

Cambridge University Press wishes to make clear that the book, unless originally published
by Cambridge, is not being republished by, in association or collaboration with, or
with the endorsement or approval of, the original publisher or its successors in title.

THE

RELIGIONS OF THE WORLD

AND THEIR

RELATIONS TO CHRISTIANITY,

CONSIDERED IN

EIGHT LECTURES

FOUNDED BY THE RIGHT HON. ROBERT BOYLE.

BY

FREDERICK DENISON MAURICE, M.A.,

CHAPLAIN OF LINCOLN'S INN, AND
PROFESSOR OF DIVINITY IN KING'S COLLEGE, LONDON.

Τὸ γνωστὸν τοῦ Θεοῦ φανερόν ἐστιν ἐν αὐτοῖς· ὁ γὰρ
Θεὸς αὐτοῖς ἐφανέρωσε.—Romans i. 19.

LONDON:

JOHN W. PARKER, WEST STRAND.

M.DCCC.XLVII.

RIGHT HONOURABLE AND RIGHT REVEREND

THE LORD BISHOP OF LONDON.

My Lord,

Through your Lordship's kindness I was appointed to the Boyle Lectureship; the same kindness has permitted me to relinquish it at the end of one year. I take the liberty of presenting to your Lordship the Discourses of that year. The study of the subject which is considered in them has been most interesting and comforting to myself; I shall be· thankful indeed if it should prove of any use to my countrymen. Desiring for the Church universal, for that portion of it especially over which your Lordship presides, and for your Lordship personally all the blessings of this season,

I have the honour to be,

My Lord,

Your Lordship's very obliged Servant,

F. D. MAURICE.

December, 1846.

CONTENTS

PART I.

LECTURE I.

PART II.

LECTURE V.

PREFACE.

THE substance of these Lectures was delivered, according to the directions of Boyle's Will, in one of the London Churches, on the first Mondays of certain months in the last and present year. Though it is not imperative on the preacher to print his Discourses, it has been the custom to do so. Indeed the intention of the founder seems to be scarcely fulfilled by addressing a series of Sermons on subjects requiring some attention, at distant intervals, to the eight or ten persons who in the present times compose an ordinary week-day congregation. In preparing them for publication I have omitted the texts, which were little more than mottoes, and have altered the forms of language which belong especially to pulpit composition.

The object of the Lectures will, I hope, be sufficiently intelligible to those who read them. But it is a duty to speak of some writers who have discussed the same subjects, and to whom I am indebted.

In the first Lecture I have not touched upon the question which is considered in Mr. Forster's *Mahometanism Unveiled.* My business was with popular views upon the subject, not with learned and ingenious speculations. Of Mr. Forster's theory I do not feel competent to express an opinion; so far as it evinces a desire to deal fairly with facts which Christian apologists have often perverted, and a confidence, that the cause of Christianity must be the better for such fairness, it must, I am sure, have done good, even if the basis upon which it rests should be found untenable.

Mr. Carlyle's Lecture on Mahomet in his *Hero Worship*, is probably much better known to my readers than Mr. Forster's treatise. Some persons may have been led by that Lecture to identify Mahometanism with reverence for the person of Mahomet; they will strongly object to the sentiments which I have expressed in one passage of this book. But I do not anticipate any such objection from Mr. Carlyle himself. No writer has more distinctly recognized the Islamite principle of subjection to an absolute Will as the vital one in this faith; or has exhibited a more earnest, I had nearly said, a more exclusive, veneration for that principle. A man seems to him to be strong or weak, admirable or contemptible, precisely as he is possessed by it or as he substitutes some notion of happiness, some theory of the Universe, in place of it. Those who feel that they are under the deepest obligation to Mr. Carlyle for the power with which he has brought the truth of this principle to their minds, for the proofs which he has given, that as much in the seventeenth century as in the seventh, it could break down whatever did not pay it homage, cannot be persuaded to look upon any phrases of his which appear to convey an opposite impression, however much they may be quoted, however partial he may seem to them himself, as the most genuine expressions of his mind. They rather recognize in the phrases an attempt, confessedly unsuccessful, to bridge over the chasm which separates, as Mr. Carlyle thinks, the ages in which this faith could be acted out from

our own in which it has become only a name. That
no phrases or formulas, from whatever period or
country they may be borrowed, can accomplish this
object, Mr. Carlyle is a sufficient witness; that it
must be accomplished in some way, his lamentations
over the present state of the world abundantly prove.
Those who think that it is the first duty of an author
to provide them with sunshine, find these lamentations intolerable; there are some who seem to be
pleased with them as they might be with any un-
usually strong exhibition of passion upon the stage.
There are others who hear in his wailings the echoes
of their own saddest convictions, but who for that
reason cannot be content to spend their time merely
in listening to them or repeating them. For one who
desires to lead an honest life, and learns that men
in former days were honest, because they believed in
a Personal Being, who is, and was, and is to come,
must ask himself whether such a belief has become
impossible for him.   And if we are assured by Mr.
Carlyle that under the conditions of Mahometanism
or even of Christian Puritanism it is now impossible,
then we must again ask, Why so ? Is it because the
truth which made these faiths so energetic is not
what it was, or is it because it dwelt in them apart
from other truths, without which in our days, it
can scarcely even exist, much less live? These
questions may never present themselves to a dilettante admirer of Mr. Carlyle ; those whom his
writings have really moved, and who regard him
with hearty, though perhaps silent, gratitude and
affection, are, I know, haunted by them continually.
If these Lectures should lead any one such ques-

tioner even to hope for an answer, they will do the
work for which I especially designed them.

In illustration of the remark that the Mahometan conquerors were not *merely* 'Scourges of God,'
however they may have deserved that title, I would
suggest to the reader a comparison of their wars
with those of Zinghis Khan. May I advise him also
to read with some attention the passage in Gibbon
(Chap. LXIV. Vol. XI. pp. 391, 392, 8vo Ed.) on the philosophical religion of that Mogul whom Frederic II.,
the accomplished Suabian, the enemy of Popes, the
suspected infidel, denounced as the common foe of
mankind, against whom he invoked a crusade of all
princes ? Gibbon's panegyric, illustrated as it is by
his faithful narrative of the proceedings of Zinghis
Khan and his successors in Persia, Russia, Hungary,
&c.; of their incapacity to preserve a record of their
own acts, and of their ultimate conversion by the bi-
gotted Mussulman, is full of the deepest instruction.

In connexion with the remarks upon the consti-
tution of Mahometan Society as exhibited in the
Ottoman Empire, I would recommend the study of
Ranke's excellent Essay upon that subject in his
Fürsten und Volken.

The second Lecture is a collection of hints,
which may not, I hope, be quite useless to some
whose personal observation of India, or whose knowledge of its languages may enable them to detect
my mistakes, and if they please, to laugh at my
ignorance. The scholars of British India and the
intelligent natives have good right to despise any
one who sets up his own notions in opposition to
their testimonies, and who makes these notions an

excuse for severe reflections upon a state of society
with which he is unacquainted. They may possibly
be tolerant of one who by comparing their testimonies, so far as he has been able to gather them,
has corrected many crude notions which he had previously entertained *, and who desires nothing more
than that any sentiments of disgust and contempt
which Englishmen in India may conceive for the
notions and practices which they witness, should
rather be counteracted than strengthened by their
English education. Professor H. Wilson has undertaken an edition of Mr. Mill's *History of British
India*, in the hope, as he intimates in his preface,
of correcting, by the evidence of facts, the harsh
judgments of the Hindoos, into which the historian,
he thinks, was led by theory. To the civil and
military servants of the Company such a work may
be as useful as the design of it is benevolent. But
the missionary, though it is to be hoped he will not
neglect to profit either by Mr. Mill's labours, or by
the experience and oriental wisdom with which Professor Wilson has enriched them, is open to another
kind of temptation, which the one will not much
increase, nor the other enable him to resist. The
actual sight of a country wholly given to idolatry,

---

* It is possible that some readers of this book, may have met with
an article on Moral and Metaphysical Philosophy, which I wrote
several years ago in the *Encyclopedia Metropolitana*. From the
principles of that article generally, I have not seen any reason to
depart ; but the few passages in it which refer to Indian life and
philosophy, seem to me very unsatisfactory and erroneous. They are
quite at variance with those I have expressed in the third and fourth
Lectures of this course.

must be far more startling and appalling to him
than any pictures he can have formed of it previously. Not to weaken these impressions, but to
prevent them from overwhelming him, and so destroying that sympathy with the victims of idolatry,
which is the most necessary qualification for his task,
should be the great object of his home instructors.
For this end, I think, we should aim, not merely at
cultivating Christian love and pity in his heart:
these will scarcely be kept alive, if there be not
also an intellectual discipline, (I call it *intellectual*,
yet it is in the very highest sense a moral discipline,)
to shew him what the thoughts and feelings of which
Hindooism is the expression, have to do with himself, how they are interpreted by the experience of
individuals and the history of the world. I look
earnestly to St. Augustine's College, in the hope
that it may fulfil both these tasks. Should it do
so, it will be indeed worthy of its name; it may
be the instrument of restoring faith to England
as well as of imparting it to her dependencies.
For do *we* not need, as I have hinted in my last
Lecture, to be taught that the Gospel is not a dead
letter, by discovering what living wants there are in
us, and all men, which it meets and satisfies?

It might have been desirable that I should have
appended to this, and the two following Lectures,
some illustrative notes: I had intended to do so,
but I feared that I should increase the size and price
of the volume, without conferring a proportionate
benefit upon the reader. I can enumerate in a few
lines the books from which my proofs would have
been drawn. From them (and they are within the

reach of persons who are as ignorant of Oriental
literature as I am,) much more may be learnt in
the course of a few hours' fair study, than from
long appendices of extracts, selected at the pleasure
of an Author.

The Essay of Mr. Colebrooke on the Vedas, in
the eighth volume of the *Asiatic Researches*, and Mr.
Rosèn's Latin translation of the *Rig Veda*, are at present* the chief helps which the Western student possesses for a knowledge of the earliest Hindoo faith.
It is important to observe, that while Mr. Colebrooke's
extracts are chiefly taken from the liturgical part of
the Vedas, those upon which the late Rammohun Roy
raised his argument for the corruption of the later
faith, were doctrinal passages.   His conclusion, as I
have hinted in my Lecture, is therefore unsatisfactory,
though it ought not to be called unfair or disinge-
nuous.   If he had quoted the prayers which Mr. Colebrooke has made us acquainted with, English readers
would no doubt have discredited his boast of the
primitive Monotheism of his country.   But they would
have done so hastily.   Those prayers imply *a* Monotheism as certainly as the direct teaching; and
the one may justly be adduced as the interpretation
of the other.   The question is, *what* Monotheism?
The prayers and doctrine I think make the same
answer: a Monotheism which made it impossible to

----

* I understand that a young German, now in London, whose
knowledge of Sanscrit is profound, and his industry *plus quàm Ger-
manica*, has it in contemplation to publish and translate all the Vedas.
English money it is to be hoped will not be wanting, when the other
and more indispensable requisite is supplied by a foreigner.

distinguish the object worshipped from the mind of
the worshipper, and *therefore* which implicitly contained, and out of which was inevitably developed,
the later Polytheism.   We may be thankful to Rammohun Roy for helping us to detect the old faith at
the root of one which seems so unlike it, but cannot
allow him to confuse us, however innocently, by
the use of a phrase, which is susceptible of the most
opposite significations.

The translation of the Menù Code, by Sir W.
Jones, brings that part of the subject within the
reach of all.   I hope the reader will verify the account I have given of it by examining it for himself,
together with the excellent digest of it, in the first
volume of Mr. Elphinstone's history.

The third Appendix to the history of this eminent statesman contains an admirable commentary
upon the Greek accounts of India, contained in
the fifteenth book of Strabo, and the *Indica* of
Arrian.

The Vishnu Purana, edited by Professor Wilson,
exhibits another and much more recent stage of the
mythology—that which I have spoken of as produced by the artificial incorporation of the old faith
with the different kinds of worship which had arisen
from popular movements and reactions. To trace the
progress of these movements with little help from
external history, is of course difficult; no one solution of the problem can be certain; all as hints may
be useful.   The one I have supposed seems to be in-
ternally probable and consistent; still there is an
objection to it which I have no wish to conceal.
Professor Wilson offers reasons for thinking that the

Puranas which have the Siva* element predominant
in them, are considerably older than those which
have the Vaishnava characteristics. It may hence
be concluded that the Siva worship itself pre-
ceded that of Vishnù. If this were the case, I
should be wrong in my fancy respecting the first
transition from the merely abstracted Brahminical
religion to the popular; at least, wrong in assuming
what may have been true in a particular case, as
explaining the history generally. Other authorities
think that the two forms of worship may have had
a contemporaneous development in different places;
a view not incompatible with the one I have taken,
especially as it is assumed on all hands that the
names considered as attributes or characters of the
divinity, as forms through which he was beheld, existed almost in the first stage of the religion.

The subject of the Philosophical sects among the
Hindoos, is treated by Mr. Colebrooke in a series of
papers in the first and second Volumes of the *Royal
Asiatic Transactions*. These papers (which should be
compared with the paper on the Védánta System, by
Col. Vans Kennedy, Vol. III. p. 412) are full of interest.

These writings of actual observers should, I
think, be studied before the speculations of even
the most intelligent thinkers. But I should be un-
grateful if I did not say that the passages on India
in the Mythologies of Baur and Windischmann, and

---

* I must beg the reader to correct the spelling of this name in
the Second and Third Lectures. It was overlooked in the correction
of one sheet, and foolishly preserved afterwards, for the sake of
consistency.

still more in Hegel's *Philosophy of History*, with the little book of Frederick Schlegel, called *Die Indien*, have illuminated many dark and dull reports, and have enabled me to feel the connexion between the thoughts of other periods and countries and those which characterise our own times.

The temptation to speak of Buddhism merely or chiefly in this connexion, is one which I was aware of when I entered upon it, in my third Lecture, and which I have striven to resist. I am sure that any advantage that we may derive from a comparison of the difficulties which have beset Asiatics in different ages, with those which are besetting Europeans now, must depend upon the earnestness with which we determine, first to understand the former in themselves. If we are more eager to make applications, than to ascertain what we have to apply, we may write a polemical treatise which will convince all who agreed with us before and will furnish writers in reviews, who have exhausted their old arguments of invective against some opponent, with a set of new phrases; but we shall not remove one perplexity from any earnest mind; we shall only throw into it a new element of confusion. The ultimate tendencies of Buddhism to entire evaporation, to mere negation, are manifest enough. The like tendencies assuredly exist, perhaps are becoming stronger every day, in Christendom. But to take the result of a certain doctrine or habit of mind, without considering its stages, varieties, counteractions; its lights as well as its shadows; how it weaves for itself at one time a dogmatic or sacerdotal vesture; how it sinks at another into a

mere speculation; above all, what an Eternal Verity
keeps it alive in all its forms; is not using it for
the warning and instruction of men, but turning it
into a mask for frightening children. If it is well
for us to show what possibilities lurk in Buddhism
because they lurk in us, still more ought we
to consider its actual history, because it is the
history of a process which may be passing in the
minds of persons whom we are most ready to
think of as having reached the last development
of unbelief; because it may be going on in us
when we are giving ourselves credit for the greatest
amount of faith.

Entering upon the subject with these feelings,
I desired to hear of Buddhism not in digests, which
represented it as a system at rest, but from intelligent observers who saw it in motion and described its different appearances. The papers on
the subject in the Royal Asiatic Society are for
this purpose invaluable, especially those of Mr.
Hodgson, to which I have referred in the text
(*Transactions*, Vol. ii. p. 222); that on Buddha and
the Phrabat by Captain Low (Vol. iii. p. 57); that on
the consecration of priests by Mr. Knox (Vol. iii.
p. 271); the disputations respecting Caste by a
Buddhist (Vol. iii. p. 160). To these may be added
different accounts of the Lama in *Asiatic Researches*,
(Vol. i. p. 197, and xvii. pp. 522—524,) and the later
narrative of Mr. Turner. For a general statement,
I know nothing better than the article on Buddhism,
in the *Penny Cyclopædia*. Dr. Pritchard's works will
supply valuable information upon this as upon most
other subjects. Of course it would be absurd to

slight the French writers upon Buddhism, though
on a subject which offers such facilities for systematising, and in which systematising is so likely
to mislead, it may be lawful to view them with some
suspicion.

Of the Confucian doctrine, on the other hand, they
are probably the best, as they are the most zealous and
enthusiastic expounders. The *Quatre Livres* of Confucius, translated by Pothier, is a moderately-sized
and readable book, and the preface to it is very useful
and instructive. The Chinese reverence of paternal
authority is abundantly illustrated in the fourth volume
of the *Mémoires sur les Chinois, par les Missionaires
de Pekin*. All our recent writers, Davis, Medhurst,
Gutzlaff, though valuable in reference to China generally, are rather vague and unsatisfactory on the
subject of its religion. The Chinese exhibition at
Knightsbridge is, in this respect, more valuable than
any of them.

The recent interpretation of the arrow-headed
inscriptions at Persepolis by Major Rawlinson will
add, no doubt, greatly to our knowledge of the
Persian or Zend doctrines. They seem to confirm
the opinion which was so long entertained upon other
grounds, that Darius Hystaspes was an instrument in
the restoration of the true Persian faith, after it had
been subverted by the Pseudo Smerdis. I tseems
also clearer than it was before, that the reformation,
which is connected with the name of Zoroaster,
consisted mainly in the assertion of the absolute
supremacy of Ormuzd. It does not follow that
Ahriman worship was prohibited or wholly denounced :
that it was continually reappearing in the popular

mind, is evident. The later Magian faith may have
been an attempt to reconcile the reformed with
the popular doctrine; or rather, may it not be supposed, that Zoroaster's was the regal creed, and that
the priests never more than partially recognized it?

What has been said respecting the three cycles of
Egyptian gods, is explained at large in the *Ægypten*
of Chevalier Bunsen, Vol. I. p. 423—433. He has
a remark (p. 432) upon the mistaken effort to form
Triads in different mythologies, by bringing together
gods from different localities, or periods of history,
which I have found very useful. Keeping it in
memory, I think I have learnt more to find in THE
Triad, an interpretation of all mythology, than if I
had laboured ever so diligently to find parallels for
it in the external parts of the systems.

If I had been writing a history instead of a
lecture, it would have behoved me, when speaking of
the relations of Christianity with Persia, to have
noticed the Nestorian missions in that country. I
believe the history of these missions would throw an
important light upon the whole subject; but it would
have led me into many details, which, especially in a
recapitulation, I was anxious to avoid. To pass over
any facts merely because they might tend to the
honour of heretics, would be grossly inconsistent
with the professions, and, I hope, with the spirit of
these Lectures*.

---

* I ought perhaps to have noticed two large Works, written by
Englishmen, on the subject of my Second Lecture; the Hindoo Antiquities of Mr. Thomas Maurice, and the work on the Literature,
Manners, and Religion of the Hindoos, by Mr. Ward. They illustrate
two habits of mind directly opposite to each other; almost equally

unfavourable, I think, to a true apprehension of the Brahminical faith, and of its relation to Christianity. Mr. Maurice seems to regard the abominations of idolatry as objects merely of literary interest and antiquarian curiosity. Mr. Ward can see only the hateful and the devilish; of what good it may be the counterfeit, what divine truth may be concealed in it, and may be needed to supplant it, he has not courage to enquire. Each, I think, is refuted on its own ground. Dilettante scholarship is found not to be sound scholarship. That which has no hold on the present, proves not to be true of the past. Mere observers of evil do not describe the evil accurately or vividly enough; the points may be correct, but the impression is false; for want of light, we do not feel the darkness. I believe most persons find it exceedingly difficult to read either of these books; quite impossible, to remember them.

I ought to have said, when speaking of Rammohun Roy, that his Tracts were written originally for his own countrymen, not for Englishmen. They were first printed in Calcutta: collected and re-published in London, I believe under his direction, in 1832.

LECTURE I.

In the year 1691 ROBERT BOYLE directed by a
Codicil to his Will "that eight Sermons should
be preached each year in London for proving the
Christian Religion against notorious Infidels, to
wit, Atheists, Theists, Pagans, Jews and Mahometans; not descending lower to any controversies
that are among Christians themselves." He desired
" that the preacher of these Sermons should be
assisting to all companies, and encouraging of them
in any undertaking for propagating the Christian
Religion to foreign parts;" and " further, that he
should be ready to satisfy such real scruples as any
may have concerning these matters, and to answer
such objections and difficulties as may be started,
to which good answers have not yet been made."

The second of these clauses seems to explain
the intention of the first. The objections to Christianity urged by Jews, Pagans and Mahometans,
were not, perhaps, likely to perplex an ordinary
Englishman. But England, in the 17th century,
was becoming more and more a colonizing country.
The American settlements were increasing in importance every year. The East India Company
had already begun its career of commerce, if not
of conquest. In his own particular department of

natural science Boyle observed the most steady
progress; no one was doing more to accelerate
it than himself. He would naturally divine, that
an advancement, not less remarkable, must take
place in another course, in which the interests of
men were far more directly engaged. He must
have felt how much the student in his closet was
helping to give speed to the ships of the merchant,
and to discover new openings to his ambition. As
a benevolent man he could not contemplate ac-
cessions to the greatness and resources of his country,
without longing that she might also be conscious
of her responsibility, that she might bring no people within the circle of her government whom
she did not bring within the circle of her Light.
Accordingly, we find him offering frequent encou-
ragement by his pen and purse to the hard-working
missionaries who were preaching the Gospel among
the North American Indians. Cheering words, pe-
cuniary help, and faithful prayers, might be all
which these teachers of savages could ask from
their brethren at home. But Boyle knew that
difficulties which they would rarely encounter must
continually present themselves to those who came
in contact with the Brahmin in Hindostan, with the
Mussulman both in Europe and Asia, with the
Jew in every corner of the globe. A man who
thought lightly or contemptuously of any of these,
or of their arguments—who had not earnestly considered what they would have to say, and what
he had to tell them—could not be expected to do

them much good. Moreover, Boyle was too well
acquainted with philosophical men, with the general
society of England, and with his own heart, not
to be aware that there was another kind of opposition more formidable than this, which the pro-
posal to diffuse Christianity abroad must struggle
with. Was the gift worth bestowing? Were we
really carrying truth into the distant parts of the
earth when we were carrying our own faith into
them? Might not the whole notion be a dream
of our vanity? Might not particular soils be adapted
to particular religions? and might not the effort
to transplant one into another involve the necessity
of mischievous forcing, and terminate in inevitable
disappointment? Might not a better day be at
hand, in which all religions alike should be found
to have done their work of partial good, of greater
evil, and when something much more comprehensive and satisfactory should supersede them?
Were not thick shadows overhanging Christendom
itself, which must be scattered before it could be
the source of light to the world?

Such questions as these Boyle must often have
heard propounded by others; but the deepest and
most painful suggestion of them had been to himself. He tells us, in the sketch of an European
tour written under the name of *Philaretus*, that
" when he was still a young man, after he had visited
" other places, his curiosity at last led him to those
" wild mountains where the first and chiefest of
" the Carthusian abbeys is seated; where the devil,

" taking advantage of that deep raving melancholy
" befitting so sad a place, his humour, and the strange
" stories and pictures he found there of Bruno, the
" father of that order, suggested such strange and
" hideous thoughts, and such distracting doubts of
" some of the fundamentals of Christianity, that
" though his looks did little betray his thoughts,
" nothing but the forbiddingness of self-dispatch
" hindered his acting it.   But, after a tedious lan-
" guishment of many months in this tedious per-
" plexity, at last it pleased God one day he had
" received the Sacrament to restore unto him the
" withdrawn sense of his favour.   But, though Phi-
" laretus ever looked upon these impious suggestions
" rather as temptations to be resisted than as doubts
" to be resolved, yet never did these fleeting clouds
" cease now and then to darken the clearest serenity
" of his quiet; which made him often say that
" injections of this nature were such a disease to the
" faith as toothache is to the body, for though it be
" not mortal, it is very troublesome.   However, as all
" things work together for good to them that love
" God, Philaretus derived from this anxiety the
" advantage of groundedness in his religion; for
" the perplexity his doubts created obliged him to
" remove them—to be seriously inquisitive of the
" truth of the very fundamentals of Christianity,
" and to hear what both Jews and Turks, and the
" chief sects of Christians, could allege for their
" several opinions; that so, though he believed more
" than he could comprehend, he might not believe

" more than he could prove, and not owe the sted-
" fastness of his faith to so poor a cause as the
" ignorance of what might be objected against it.
" He said, speaking of those persons who want not
" means to enquire and abilities to judge, that it
" was not a greater happiness to inherit a good
" religion, than it was a fault to have it only by
" inheritance, and think it the best because it is
" generally embraced, rather than embrace it be-
" cause we know it to be the best. That though
" we cannot always give a reason for what we be-
" lieve, yet we should be ever able to give a reason
" why we believe it. That it is the greatest of follies
" to neglect any diligence that may prevent the
" being mistaken where it is the greatest of miseries
" to be deceived. That how dear soever things taken
" upon the score are sold, there is nothing worse
" taken up upon trust than religion, in which he
" deserves not to meet with the true one that
" cares not to examine whether or no it be so."
(Works, Vol. I., p. 12.)

It is evident, I think, that a comparison of
religious systems undertaken by a man who had
just passed through so tremendous a conflict, and
who had no professional motive for entering upon
it, must have been something very different from
a dry legal enquiry respecting the balance of pro-
babilities in favour of one or the other. I do not
mean that Boyle will not have brought to this
subject all the habits of patient investigation which
he ordinarily applied to the study of physical

phenomena. The very anguish of his mind made
it essential that he should seek for a real standing
ground; and that he should not therefore strain
facts for the sake of arriving at an agreeable conclusion. Indeed, it is difficult to say which conclusion would seem most agreeable to a man exercised as he was: there would be at times a bias of
understanding, and even affection, as strong against
Christianity, as his education could create in favour
of it. But, undoubtedly, his object in questioning
these different schemes of belief will have been
to ascertain what each of them could do for him;
what there was in it to meet the demands of his
heart and reason. It was no occasion for clever
special pleading; the question was to him one
of life and death: when he had once resolved it,
the next duty was to act upon his conviction, and
to strive that all men should be better for that,
which he, because he was a man, had found to
be needful for himself. Upon this principle he
founded these Lectures. The truth of which he
had become assured, was, he believed, a permanent
one; the next generation would need it as much
as his own. He did not suppose that the actual
relation in which that truth stood to different
systems of belief could alter. But it did not follow
that the enquiry respecting the nature of that
relation would be exhausted in his day. As new
regions unfolded themselves to European adventure,
new facts, modifying or changing previous notions
respecting the faiths which prevailed in them, might

come to light; fresh and more trying experiences might make the past more intelligible; the same doubts respecting the justice, wisdom, or possibility of bringing other men into our religious fellowship which presented themselves to his contemporaries, might appear again and again in very different shapes, and appealing to even opposite feelings and tempers.

The event, I believe, has proved that he was right. Within fifty years a prodigious change has taken place in the feelings of men generally—of philosophical men particularly — respecting Religious Systems. In the latter part of the 17th century, still more during a great part of the 18th, they were regarded by those who most gave the tone to popular thinking, and who had the highest reputation for wisdom, as the inventions of lawgivers and priests. Men cleverer and more dishonest than the rest of the world, found it impossible to build up systems of policy, or to establish their own power, unless they appealed to those fears of an invisible world, which ignorance so willingly receives, and so tenderly fosters. This being the admitted maxim respecting religions generally, it seemed the office of the Christian apologist to shew that there was one exception; to explain why the Gospel could not be referred to this origin; how entirely unlike it was to those forms of belief which were rightly considered deceptions. That many dangerous positions were confuted by works written with this object; that many of the dis-

tinguishing marks of Christianity were brought
out in them; that many learnt from them to seek
and to find a standing-ground in the midst of
pits and morasses, it is impossible to doubt. But
the demonstrations of God's providence were in
this case, as in all others, infinitely broader, deeper,
more effectual than those of man's sagacity. The
evidence furnished by the great political Revolution at the close of the last century, seems slowly
to have undermined the whole theory respecting
the invisible world, and men's connection with
it, which possessed the teachers of that century.
Men are beginning to be convinced, that if Religion
had had only the devices and tricks of statesmen
or priests to rest upon, it could not have stood
at all; for that these are very weak things indeed,
which, when they are left to themselves, a popular
tempest must carry utterly away. If they have
lasted a single day, it must have been because they
had something better, truer than themselves, to sustain them. This better, truer thing, it seems to be
allowed, must be that very faith in men's hearts
upon which so many disparaging epithets were
cast, and which it was supposed could produce no
fruits that were not evil and hurtful. Faith it
is now admitted has been the most potent instrument of good to the world; has given to it nearly all
which it can call precious. But then it is asked,
is there not ground for supposing that all the
different religious systems, and not one only, may
be legitimate products of that faith which is so

essential a part of man's constitution? Are not they manifestly adapted to peculiar times and localities and races? Is it not probable that the theology of all alike is something merely accidental, an imperfect theory about our relations to the universe, which will in due time give place to some other? Have we not reason to suppose that Christianity, instead of being, as we have been taught, a revelation, has its root in the heart and intellects of man, as much as any other system? Are there not the closest the most obvious relations between it and them? Is it not subject to the same law of decay from the progress of knowledge and society with all the rest? Must we not expect that it too will lose all its mere theological characteristics, and that what at last survives of it will be something of a very general character — some great ideas of what is good and beautiful—some excellent maxims of life, which may very well assimilate, if they be not actually the same, with the essential principles which are contained in all other religions, and which will also, it is hoped, abide for ever.

Notions of this kind will be found, I think, in much of the erudite as well of the popular literature of this day; they will often be heard in social circles; they are undoubtedly floating in the minds of us all. While they hover about us, it is clearly impossible that we can, with sound hearts and clear consciences, seek to evangelize the world: yet they are not to be spoken of as if they proceeded from a mere denying, unbelieving spirit: they are

often entertained by minds of deepest earnestness;
they derive their plausibility from facts which
cannot be questioned, and which a Christian should
not wish to question. They may, I believe, if
fairly dealt with, help to strengthen our own convictions, to make our duty plainer, and to shew
us better how we shall perform it. All their
danger lies in their vagueness: if we once bring
them fairly to those tests by which the worth of
hypotheses in another department is ascertained,
it may not perhaps be hard to discover what portions of truth, and what of falsehood, they contain. I think I shall be carrying out the intention of Boyle's Will, if I attempt, in my present
course, to make this experiment. I propose to
examine the great Religious Systems which present themselves to us in the history of the world,
not going into their details, far less searching
for their absurdities; but enquiring what was their
main characteristical principle. If we find, as the
objectors say, good in each of them, we shall desire
to know what this good is, and under what conditions it may be preserved and made effectual.
These questions may, I think, be kept distinct from
those which will occupy us in the latter half of the
course. In what relation does Christianity stand
to these different faiths? If there be a faith which
is meant for mankind is this the one, or should
we look for another?

I shall not take these systems in their historical order, but rather according to the extent of

the influence they have exerted over mankind; a
reason which would at once determine me to begin
in the present Lecture with MAHOMETANISM.

For the first ninety years after the publication
of this religion in the world, the Christians of
Europe could do little more than wonder at its
amazing and, as it seemed, fatal progress in Asia
and Africa. Before the end of the century it had
obtained a settlement in a corner of their own Continent, and threatened every part of it. But the
new Western Empire established itself, Christian
champions appeared in Spain, the power of the
Caliphs declined. Then Islamism appeared again
in another conquering, proselytising tribe. For two
centuries the European nations wrestled to recover
its conquests in the Holy Land. A period followed
during which the disciples of both religions seemed
almost equally threatened by Tartar hordes. These
stooped to the Crescent; in the ·15th century a
mighty Mahometan government was seen occupying
the · capital of the East, threatening the Latin
world, profiting by the disputes of Christian sove-
reigns with one another, exhibiting its own order
and zeal in melancholy contrast to the quarrels,
unbelief, and heartlessness of monarchs and pre-
lates. It became a question with the thoughtful
men of that time, whether the Ottoman empire
did not possess a polity which was free from the
tendencies to weakness and decay that had existed
in all previous governments, and whether it might
not last for ever.

In the 17th and 18th centuries, when the fallacy of this notion was making itself evident, Christians began to speculate coldly and quietly upon the causes which had given such prevalency to this faith in past days, and which still kept it alive in their own. It may be well to consider a few of the explanations which different persons, according to their different observations or habits of mind, have offered of this fact, that we may not lose the benefit of any light which has been thrown from any quarter upon the nature or principle of the religion itself.

I. It was an easy and obvious method of solving the difficulty, to say that the Mahometans had triumphed by the force of their arms; personal valour, and a compact military organization being comprehended under that term. That they were warriors from the very first, that their courage was often amazing, and that the Ottomans for a very long time possessed the secret of military subordination, more than almost any nation has ever possessed it, is evidently true. And it is a truth of which Christian apologists would very naturally avail themselves. The opposition, not in some accidental points, but in its whole scheme and conception, between the Sermon on the Mount, and the doctrine which could require or sanction such methods for its diffusion, would of course be carefully noted. Plain men would be asked to declare which teaching bore clearest tokens of belonging to the earth, which of a Divine origin.

Nor was this argument an unfair one, however
it might be, and has been again and again, traversed by an appeal to the practice of Christians,
and the weapons to which they have resorted for
the defence and propagation of their faith.   For
it is quite clear that the Mahometan wars are
no accidental outgrowth of the system—that they
were not resorted to with a doubtful conscience,
with any uneasy feeling that they might by possibility be inconsistent with the intentions of their
Founder.   On the contrary, the very spirit and
life of Mahometanism exhibited themselves in these
wars.   In them came forth all the most striking
and characteristic virtues which the doctrine has
a right to boast of.

The Mahometan ruler felt that he was fulfilling
his vocation, when he was going forth against the
infidel; he could scarcely fulfil it in any other
way.   We know indeed that Bagdad and Cordova
became celebrated for all graceful refinements, for
letters, even for toleration.   We know that science,
physical and metaphysical, became distinctive marks
of the Arabians.   Where a book like the Koran,
written in a beautiful language, is regarded with
unbounded reverence, by degrees it will be studied;
and out of that study will be produced a literature which may spread itself in various directions.
Monarchs would feel the influence of such pursuits,
and would consider it their chief honour to direct
them.   But though periods like those of Haroun-
al-Raschid were sure to occur in the history of

Mahometanism, though in one sense they may
be considered natural developments of it, they
assuredly do not belong to the religion as such;
they rather shewed that the original spirit which
possessed its disciples was becoming feeble; they
portended a further decline of it, and probably its
revival in some more vigorous form. Whenever
a Mahometan ruler quite allows his arms to rust,
whenever he does not feel that it is his main work
in the world to diffuse his doctrine by those means
which are most simple and direct, we may be sure,
whatever temporary prosperity may be vouchsafed
him, that his dynasty cannot last very long.

But though on these grounds it may be fair to
represent Mahometanism as essentially warlike, it
is surely a great mistake to suppose that by saying
so, we have accounted for its spread over so large
a portion of the earth. No thoughtful man could
accept such a solution, because when he hears of
valour in men and discipline in armies, he must
ask himself whence these proceeded, how they came
to attach themselves to this particular faith; and
because that question must inevitably lead him to
seek for the real ground of success elsewhere. It
cannot satisfy any Christian, because the very belief
which he opposes to that of the Mahometan, must
teach him that arms are not the most mighty
things; that there are secret invisible influences
which are stronger than they.

II. The extraordinary proneness of the human
mind to embrace any imposture, was resorted to

as a second method of accounting for this phenome-
non, which might perhaps combine with the former,
and help out its weakness.   Of this proneness, the
records of the world's history seem to supply abundant proofs—our own daily experience of others, and
of ourselves, still more.   All men, in one language
or another, have confessed that there is something
in man which tempts him to embrace falsehood,
and disown truth, to follow deceitful guides, to
reject the honest and true, to make a lie, and to
love it.   And yet I think all also confess, in one
kind of language or another, that whenever any
man, or any set of men, have learnt to relish what
is false, and dislike what is true for its own sake,
that man, or that body of men, is in the last stage
of corruption and degradation—is approaching a
point in which manliness, faith, and union become
impossible—in which the death of all individual
power, of all social existence, is at hand.   That
the elements of such destruction are in every human being, and in every human fellowship, at every
moment, and that the records of religious systems
present the saddest memorials of them, none will
dispute.   But that they can ever account for
the existence of any thing which has endured for
a long time, which has manifested great power;
that in them lies the source of a vigour and con-
centration which they are perpetually threatening
to extinguish, I think no sane person who sets
the question fairly before himself can believe.   We
may need the propensity of men to believe impos-

ture, as a key to many portions of Mahometan history, to many circumstances of its present condition; we shall not find therein the secret of its diffusion and predominance.

III. Led by these, or other considerations, to feel that what is right must be recognized in this system, as well as what is wrong, Christians have sometimes explained its influence, by speaking of the plagiarisms in the Koran from the Old and New Testament Scriptures. That Mahometanism derived much from its connection with the older faiths of the world, would be confessed, I suppose, even by the philosophers who have least veneration for those faiths. They would easily acknowledge, nay, have often acknowledged, how much historical dignity and sacredness an Arabian teacher must have acquired by connecting himself with patriarchs who had lived 2000 years before; who were attached, by closest links of association, to the very soil his countrymen trod ; whose doctrine he could speak of, as the truth given to their fathers, now revived in its purity by himself. Nor would it be denied by these philosophers, that one living not only among Sabean worshippers, but amongst Christians and Jews, might advance his cause by professing his sympathy with much of the teaching in their holy books; by saying, that he came to restore their systems also to their purity, while he delivered his countrymen from their idolatry. But though, perhaps, thus much might be conceded by all, far more by a firm believer in the Bible, it may be fairly

doubted whether the word "plagiarism" is one
suited to the case; or whether, so far as Mahomet
was a mere plagiarist, he could have exerted any
influence. If he merely transferred passages from
our Scriptures to his, merely adopted formal doctrines which they set forth in living power to mix
them with his own notions, one cannot believe that
he ever would have moved the heart of a single
nation or of a single man. A teacher may, indeed,
exercise a much greater power by reviving what
is old, than by inventing what is new; but to
revive a principle he must have been penetrated
by it, it must have taken possession of him, it must
have inspired his whole being; otherwise he could
never impart it to others. Something of this sort
must have been the case with Mahomet; and therefore his plagiarisms, great as they may have been,
do not account for his success.

IV. The same answer may serve for those
persons of a very different temper who are disposed
to dwell with complacency upon passages in the
Koran which contain just and benevolent sentiments, and who believe that these were not merely
transferred from Jewish or Christian sources, but
actually exhibited the heart of the writer. We
may admit the existence of such sentiments; we
need not, in the least, wish to represent them
as insincere or hypocritical; we may believe that
they have exercised a real influence over the minds
of Mussulmans, who constantly repeat them, and
look upon them as proceeding from a prophet of

God. But we cannot believe that mere phrases
and sentiments, be they ever so good, nay, even if
they did not occur in the midst of any that are
fond, or trivial and contradictory to themselves,
could have wrought a deep conviction into the
minds of men previously indisposed to them. A
precept may be of vast weight when we have first
bowed to the preceptor; otherwise it is weak : it
may be respected and praised, but it will not be
followed; nothing will be abandoned for the sake
of it.

V. There would seem then to be far more
plausibility in the opinion of those who attribute
great weight to the character of Mahomet itself,
believing that however it may have been mixed
of good and evil qualities, it was of a kind to
act mightily upon his own countrymen, and through
them upon mankind. He has been spoken of as
one of the great governing and leavening minds
of the world, one able to stamp his own image
upon nations and generations. Men did homage
to him, it has been said, as they always will
do homage to one who they feel is their master,
who is stronger than they, because his convictions
are stronger, because he has grappled more with
realities, because he has faith in unseen substances,
of which they see little more than the shadows.
Such assertions may be at variance with many
conceptions we have formed of this man, but there
is much in his biography to bear them out; there
is nothing in them, I believe, to startle any Chris-

tian who knows the grounds of his own belief.
At what point the strong conviction of a truth
which must be divine, which must be given us
from above, becomes mixed with self-exaltation,
with the desire of shewing how wise we are, and
of exercising a dominion over others for our own
sakes, it is hard to determine in any case. The
more we know of ourselves, the more we shall
understand how it is possible to vibrate between
a certainty we have of principles, which for the
sake of our moral being we cannot part with,
and a positiveness about notions which we have
grounded upon them. When the conscience is
clear, when the man is lowly, when he has been
subdued by discipline, the opposition seems clear to
him as between day and night; the delusion of his
own heart is manifested to him by the light which
God has kindled there. But amidst the noise of
human applause the distinction which was so
definite vanishes, the precious and the vile become
hopelessly mingled. Such personal experiences,
which all have had in a greater or less degree—
which earnest and thoughtful young men especially
often require to be schooled in, because it depends
upon the way they use them whether strong and
clear and bright impressions in their minds shall
destroy their docility, shall make them merely
utterers of some new notion, or shall ripen into
blessed discoveries of that which is true—these
experiences, I say, may help us to read the bio-
graphies of men who have had a great influence

upon the world, with a kindlier and truer feeling.
Their impressions were, doubtless, more overpower-
ing than ours, their conflicts greater, their temptations severer. It is hard to say, that because they
called themselves inspired, they meant to de-
ceive; that language might be the language of
humility, not of arrogance—the confession that
every good gift, above all, every illumination respecting any invisible reality, cometh from the Father of Lights.   Not in this conviction, but in that
pride which forgat Him—in the desire to be something in themselves—do we trace the beginning of
all imposture; in the blending of the two together,
the melancholy mixture which religious systems present to one who studies them in themselves or in
their effects. I am far then from wishing to deny
that Mahomet's character may have met with unfair treatment at the hands of Christians; and it is,
without doubt, one of the most noticeable circumstances in the history of his religion, that his own
person should have been so much bound up with
it; that every caliph or sultan who has reigned over
any tribe of his followers should have reigned in his
name; that the name of a man should have so
much more power than even the book which
Mussulmans regard with such profound reverence;
that the honour of a human chieftain should so
markedly distinguish a religion which looks upon
man as separated by such an immeasurable distance
from the object of his worship. But this last
remark shews that the person and character of

Mahomet, important as they may have been in their practical influence, cannot satisfactorily explain the charm by which his religion worked its way; in fact, it is one of the anomalies which requires to be accounted for, that a human leader should win this reverence. He himself declared and felt that he was nothing but a witness for God; his followers received and honoured him in that character. All the worth he had in him was derived from that of which he testified. When he began consciously to take up any other position it was one of weakness. We may consider Mahomet a hero if we please; we may regard the reverence for him as a proof of men's tendency in all circumstances to worship heroes; but we cannot, without denying the plainest facts of the case, say that the success of his doctrine was a consequence of this disposition. His teaching was emphatically the denial of that worship; every Mahometan sword was drawn to prove that it was false, and to put it down.

VI. It might seem to follow inevitably, from what has just been said, that the Monotheism of Mahomet, and his hatred of idolatry, constituted the strength and vitality of his system. This opinion has often been maintained, and a reader of the history is continually tempted to adopt it. As we follow any of the earlier conquerors through Persia, through Egypt, through India, through the Greek empire, we feel that the enthusiasm of the chief and the soldier is connected with what they believe to be the destruction of false worship, the carrying out of the first and second Commandment. All are regarded alike as infidels, because all are thought to have raised something *created* into the place and glory of the Creator. The belief that nothing in the earth, nothing in the heavens, not even light, is a symbol of God; that not even man himself can be looked upon in any other character than as a minister of the one Supreme Being, evidently inspires every enterprize. In the strength of it they destroy temples, idols, priests, plunder cities, make slaves of their inhabitants, turn their children into soldiers of the Crescent. All this is true, and yet I think no considerate person will suppose that mere opposition to the grossest forms of false worship could give nerve to any arm, far less permanence to any society. If Monotheism means the not believing in many gods, it could, as little as the other causes we have enumerated, be the root of the Mahometan faith, and the Mahometan power.

VII. But these sweeping conquests of Mahomet are susceptible of yet another interpretation, which has sometimes been applied to the whole history of their dominion: they may be regarded as the righteous judgments of God upon guilty nations, whether these were the idolaters of India, the fire-worshippers of Persia, the corrupted Greek, or the Visigoth. It is difficult, I should think, for

any person really taking the Bible as his guide,
nay, for any person recognizing a Divine Providence at all, not to look upon every great earth-
quake which has shaken kingdoms as a Divine
visitation; not to see a Divine hand regulating
outward circumstances, and the wills of men. Nor
can we go so far without going further, and asking
what the state of those nations was on which
the scourge descended? If we pursue the enquiry
fairly in this case, we shall be led, it seems to
me, to the discovery of the real ground of the
Mahometan might, and perhaps to regard the
continuance of that might through so many ages
(not wholly) in the light of a punishment. In
the Christian nations which were permitted to fall
under the armies of Islam, almost as much as in
those which were avowedly Pagan, the sense of
a Divine, Almighty Will, to which all human
wills were to be bowed, had evaporated amidst
the worship of outward images, moral corruptions, philosophical theories, religious controversies.
Notions about God, more or less occupied them;
but God Himself was not in all their thoughts.
The awe of an Absolute, Eternal Being, to be
obeyed as well as to be confessed, was passing
away in some—had scarcely been awakened in
others. It was given, I believe, to the soldiers of
Mahomet to make this proclamation in the ears of
men. They said, by their words and acts, "God
verily is, and man is his minister, to accomplish
his will upon earth." This we shall find was the

inspiring thought in the warriors of the Crescent—
this gave them valour, subordination, and discipline. This, where it encountered no like or
equal feeling in the minds of those among whom
they came, made them invincible. We must not
be content with talking of their armies, because
here was the life of their armies. We must not
speak of men's readiness to receive an imposture;
in yielding to this assertion they were bowing to
a truth. This was no verbal copy from older
records; it may have been the oldest of all veri-
ties, but it was fresh and new for every one who
acted upon it. It was no mere phrase out of a
book—no homage to a mortal hero—no mere denial
of other men's faith. Let us go yet farther and
say, It was a mercy of God that such a witness,
however bare of other supporting principles, however surrounded by confusions, should have been
borne to His Name, when His creatures were
ready, practically, to forget it. The first Mahometan conquests, the continued Mahometan dominion, has borne witness to this everlasting truth;
has proclaimed that it is no mere dry proposition,
that it is capable of exercising a mastery over the
rudest tribes, of giving them an order, of making
them victorious over all the civilization and the
religion which has not this principle for its basis.

I think that most persons studying the history
of Mahometanism without prejudice, will feel that
this is the principle which confronts them at every
turn, and to which everything else is subordinate.

And if so, the consideration is surely a very important one for our purpose. We are told that some great general principles are enshrined in different religious systems; that the mere theological part of these systems is nothing—a loose, flimsy drapery for certain great maxims of morality, or certain ideas about the nature and spiritual destinies of man. How does the study of Mahometanism bear out this opinion? Is it a collection of moral maxims which has been the strength of this system? Is it some theory or conception about the nature of man? Precisely the opposite assertion is true. All mere maxims, all mere ideas about the nature of man, have proved weak and helpless before this assertion of a living and Eternal God. The theological transcendant principle is just the one which has stood its ground, which has re-appeared age after age, which the most ignorant warriors felt was true and mighty for them, for which no cultivation could provide any substitute. We are told, again, that the character of particular localities and races determines what shall be the character of a theology; that that only is universal which concerns the laws of outward nature or the life of man. How does the history of Mahometanism bear out this notion? Let it be granted that the soil of Arabia was one on which it was fitting that such a doctrine as that of Mahomet should be first proclaimed: let it be allowed that the Semitic race has been especially distinguished from every other by an interest

in what is purely Divine, by a comparative indifference to what is human. But here is a truth;
one which tribes the most remote from this are
compelled to recognize; which establishes itself
in India, in Syria, in Egypt, in Greece. And
it is remarkable that, while numerous sects and
parties have been called into existence by questions respecting the proper successors of Mahomet,
or the interpretation of the Koran, the Divine principle among them has been the uniting one. It
is said again, that the great doctrines which have
been embodied in religious systems are the crea-
tions of the religious principle in man ; that his
faith moulds the object which it worships : in
other words, that what is called theological truth is
but some outward expression of our feelings or habits
of mind. Look again at the history of Mahometanism ; consider the facts steadily : there are
none to which the supporters of this theory should
more gladly appeal. They can find no other in-
stance of a race of which faith in an unseen object
was more characteristic. " Faithful " is the very
name by which the Islamite warriors proclaim
themselves to the world. But what was the nature
of this faith ? It meant nothing, it was nothing, except so far as it asserted a Being *not* dependent on itself; the ground of man's being ;
one of whom he was the minister, not the Creator.
The Mahometan believed that the God whom he
worshipped must have revealed Himself—that man
could not have discovered Him. He went forth

to beat into powder all gods which he supposed
man had invented. Take away these characteristics from his faith and it vanishes, with all the
doings which were the fruits of it.

One question still remains to be considered
before I close this Lecture. May not the principle
which Mahometanism embodies be left to the
protection of the system which it seems to have
created for itself?—We must look into Mahometan history itself for the answer.

When I spoke to you of the great power by
which the Mahometan soldier was carried along
in his enterprizes, of the principle which gave
him strength and endurance, you may have wondered that I did not dwell more upon the rewards
which were promised to him after death, of the
Paradise of sensual felicity for which the brave
man was encouraged to hope. I did not allude
to this motive, because I do not believe that it
was the one by which the Mahometan hosts were
really inspired. The mighty conviction that they
were then, at that very moment, called by God
to a work—that they were proclaiming His Name,
and were the ministers of His vengeance, was, I
believe, immeasurably more effective than any
dreams, were they ever so gross and palpable, of
what might be given to them hereafter. When
they had already cast themselves away to live or
die, they had a sense of immortality which no such
visions could impart, which alone made them credible.

But when the Mahometan was at peace, the

belief of a mighty Sovereign, to whom he was doing homage, no longer sufficed him: he began to ask himself what he was living for? To the multitude these sensual promises were a tolerable answer. These were the things to be desired; for these, by whatsoever means the Koran or its interpreters prescribed, if they were in earnest, they were to labour. Some, with higher apprehensions, would feel that such rewards were not satisfying; they would explain away the language of Mahomet, and pursue the practices to which the others submitted, in hope of earthly gratifications, that they might attain the knowledge or vision of God. The former would fall into all gross moral corruptions, the latter would be always tending to mere philosophical speculations—would be founding sects— would be substituting theories and notions for that Being in whose name their fathers had fought. This has actually been the case, and hence it has been proved that Mahometanism can only thrive while it is aiming at conquest. Why? Because it is the proclamation of a mere Sovereign, who employs men to declare the fact that he is a Sovereign, and to enforce it upon the world. It is not the proclamation of a great moral Being who designs to raise His creatures out of their sensual and natural degradation; who reveals to them not merely that He is, but *what* He is—why He has created them—what they have to do with Him. Unless this mighty chasm in the Mahometan doctrine can be filled up, it must wither day by day—

wither for all purposes of utility to mankind ; it
can leave nothing behind but a wretched carcase,
filling the air with the infection of its rottenness.

For, secondly, see how that which gave all the
dignity and glory to this system becomes, from
its want of some other element, the very cause
of its degradation. The absolute government of
the unseen Being had presented itself to the Mussulman, in every age, in the absolute, visible
government of his caliph or sultan. While the
Divine feeling was strong and alive, the subjection to the human ruler was an affectionate,
dutiful, entire submission. The ruler was, in very
deed, the centre of his warriors. He felt towards
them as a protector, sharing their toils, bound
to the same master, enduring hardships in the
same cause. But the battle over, he becomes the
absolute monarch in the midst of his seraglio—
they merely his slaves. There is no such connection between him and the Being whom he worshipped as permanently to check this tendency—
to make the monarch feel that he is set over
them to do them good, or the subjects that they
had an appeal against him to a higher Ruler.

The very nature of the Ottoman government—
and that government is the perfect developement
of the Mahometan idea—excludes the possibility
of orders and gradations in society. Its strength
lies in all being simply subjects of the one
Ruler, holding their offices not in virtue of any
hereditary ranks or privileges, but only at his plea-

sure. When therefore the one principle which quickened the whole society waxes feeble, of necessity it becomes the most intolerable of all despotisms. Elsewhere there is a balance and conflict of powers, which even in the dreariest periods produces struggles or paroxysms of life; here, if the monarch do not inspire his people with strength, all is dead. And the same cause which destroys what may be called the family bonds of civil society, destroys equally the family itself. Polygamy is no accident of Mahometanism: a careful consideration of the system will shew that it must fall to pieces the moment any reformer should attempt to remove this characteristic of it.

But again, the first principle of Mahometanism wanting the support of some other which it does not acknowledge, must change, and is continually changing, into one which is the counterfeit and direct opposite of itself. The belief of a living, acting Will passes into the acknowledgment of a dead necessity, a Fate, against which there is no struggling, which drives the soul not to energy for some great object, but to indifference, languor, and the submission that means despair. Oftentimes indeed the patience of a Turk must even yet awaken our homage and our shame. Joyfully would we confess that God has not yet suffered the true principle to be wholly extinguished by its bastard product. But we would draw from that confession not a pretext for leaving this, or any feeble and beautiful plant of a better soil, to the hot-bed which has

always impeded their growth, and now threatens
to stifle them altogether; but a certain hope that
they are intended to receive culture from without,
and that, by help of it, they may yet blossom
and bear fruit abundantly.

These remarks may prepare us to take notice
of one great fact in the history of Mahometanism,
which is the connecting link between it and the
other systems, of which I propose to speak hereafter.

I have talked of the victories of the Crescent
in the different quarters of the globe, and it is
difficult to exaggerate the greatness of those victories. Yet we all know they were not complete;
they did not exterminate that which they were
meant to exterminate. I do not speak now of the
resistance which this great power encountered from
the hammer of the Mayor of Paris, or from the
heroes in the Asturian mountains. I do not
speak of anything which is directly connected with
Christianity. I mean that the most remarkable of
the old polytheistic faiths, though crushed, were
not cast out; that some of the countries which
yielded to Mahometans are not Mahometan. It
behoves us to enquire into the meaning of this
fact—to ask ourselves what there was in their
doctrines, compounded of all strange elements,
sanctioning so many fearful crimes, for which
the simple and purer Mahometan faith could provide no satisfaction. We may find that convictions which the Mahometan trampled down, do

as much require recognition as those which he
enforced ; that man has demands for himself which
will not be satisfied by being told that he is the
servant of an absolute Will—demands which must,
somehow or other, find their explanation—must
in some way or other be reconciled with that
great truth.

I will not anticipate the nature or the results
of that enquiry ; but I hope we may gather something from the one in which we have been engaged.
You have found a set of men brought up in circumstances altogether different from yours, who
hold your faith in abhorrence, saying in language
the most solemn and decisive, " Whatever else
we part with, this is needful to us and to all
human beings, the belief that God is—the recognition of Him as a living personal Being." You
have seen this faith growing weak for a time,
and everything else growing weak with it; you
have seen it re-appearing, finding a new set of
champions to assert it, compelling nations to bow
before it. Be sure that here is something which
the heart and reason within you have need of—
which they must grasp. Be quite sure, that if
you give them in place of it any fine notions or
theories, if you feed them with phrases about
the beautiful or the godlike, when they want the
source of beauty, the living God : if you entertain
them with any images or symbols of art or nature
when they want that which is symbolized, if you
talk about physical laws when you want the law-

giver, of mechanical properties when you want him who set them in motion, of secret powers when you want him who acts by them and upon you, you are cheating yourselves—cheating mankind. Remember this further, that the acknowledgment of this Being may imply much more than the Mahometan perceived, but that it does imply *that* which he perceived. If such an One is, His will must be the law of the universe. Every creature in the universe must be in a right or wrong position, must be doing his work well, or failing in it, as he yields himself to this will, or as he resists it. And let us not fancy that the Mahometan was entirely mistaken as to the way in which this will is to be obeyed. He may not have understood *what* enemies he had to fight with, what weapons he had to wield, but he did discover that the life of man is to be a continual battle, that we are only men when we are engaging in that battle. He was right that there is something in the world which we are not to tolerate, which we are sent into it to exterminate. First of all, let us seek that we may be freed from it ourselves; but let us be taught by the Mussulman that we shall not compass this end unless we believe, and act upon the belief, that every man and every nation exists for the purpose of chasing falsehood and evil out of God's universe.

<hr />

LECTURE II.

THE remarks which I made at the close of my last Lecture will prepare you to expect that I should speak in the present of HINDOOISM. That faith has been brought into conflict with Mahometanism, has succumbed to it, and yet has maintained its ground, leaving the victorious religion the religion of a small minority. Though it may pretend to an antiquity which it does not possess, it has certainly lasted 3000 years. The language in which its holy books are composed is the mother-tongue—if I may use that phrase in its literal, rather than its ordinary sense—of the Greek, the Latin, and the dialects of our Gothic ancestors; consequently, of nearly all which are spoken in Western Europe at this day. From this fact it might, I think, be inferred, if other evidence were wanting, that the mythologies of these nations could be traced to an Indian source. But there is abundant evidence, so much as to have misled those scholars who were first struck with it into a forgetfulness of the important historical principle, that we cannot determine the character of nations, or of their belief, merely by finding the point from which they may have started; that each must be studied in itself and in its own utterances, and

that we gain only a secondary aid in our inves-
tigations when we have the means of affiliating it
to some other.   That this mistake was committed
by some of the great Orientalists of the last
century, I think is now generally acknowledged;
they seemed to suppose that they could learn more
of the Greeks from Sanscrit books than from their
own.   But an extravagance which is natural to all
discoverers does not make the discovery itself less
valuable; in fact, we are only beginning to ap-
preciate its importance.   The more practically we
learn to sympathize with our fellow-men in all
countries and in all ages, to cultivate such sympathy
for our own sake and for theirs, and for the glory
of God, the more will all such hints respecting
the relationship between different nations be reflected on and prized.   And this remark suggests
another, and much weightier reason, why a Boyle
Lecturer should address himself to the subject
of Hindooism, and why we all should take an
interest in it.   It is the faith, to say the least,
of between eighty and ninety millions of people,
subjects of the British empire.   By conquests
scarcely paralleled for rapidity in the annals of
the world, we have obtained supremacy over them,
and by civil policy we have tried to preserve it.
As to the true character of this policy there has
been the greatest variety of opinion; but I think
intelligent men are now well agreed, that whatever
it be, it must be grounded upon a knowledge of
the character, institutions, faith of the people who

are to be influenced by it. Civilians, military officers,
and missionaries in India, have exerted themselves
to acquire this knowledge, and to make it available
for us.   Their theories, as well as their facts, when
they seem most contradictory, are worthy of study
and of comparison ; they may all help us in finding
the principle of Indian life and belief, and that
principle, when we apprehend it, may make the
differences in their observations and opinions more
intelligible.

There are, unquestionably, considerable difficulties in the investigation.   This ancient people
is strictly speaking without a history.   " No date
of a public event,"—I use the words of Mr. Elphinstone,—" can be fixed before the invasion of Alexander ; no connected relation of the national transactions can be attempted until after the Mahometan
conquest." · Yet it would seem that we were in the
greatest need of such records to connect the phænomena which offer themselves to the eye of the
traveller in this day with the early books which
are still regarded with the profoundest veneration.
A Hindoo will sometimes tell us in wild language
that he acknowledges 300 millions of gods ; he
means, of course, that the number is indefinite, that
any object or power in nature, any heroic man
may be a god. And those who trace Oriental
extravagance in such a description, will, nevertheless, remember to have heard of various beings who
are acknowledged objects of Hindoo adoration—
of Brahma the Creator, of Vishnu the Preserver,

of Sheeva the Destroyer, of Indra, the Lord of the
Elements, of the fearful goddess Devi, of the
beautiful hero Krishna, and a multitude more.
Yet learned and trustworthy critics, Asiatic as well
as European, confidently affirm that the ground
of the Brahminical faith is Monotheistic; that One
Being is assumed in the earliest of the sacred books
to be the origin of all things; that this was no
lazy, inoperative tenet, that it penetrated the whole
system of worship, and the life of the worshipper.
Putting such facts and such statements together,
you might be ready to conclude that there was
no real identity between the faith of one of these
periods and of the other; that either by conquest,
or some strange process of degeneracy, the character and feelings of the people had become so
changed as to make the notion of one Hindoo or
Brahminical religion a mere delusion. But many
considerations will shew us that this opinion, however plausible, is untenable. I have said, that the
early Vedas, composed, perhaps, 1500 years before
the time of Christ, be their tenets what they may,
are still regarded with unbounded veneration by
the religious men among the Hindoos. The Menu
code or institute, which is probably about 600 or
700 years younger than these, and which indicates
some, though not radical, alterations of practice and
opinion during the interval, must still be the great
study of every English jurist who wishes to understand the grounds of Hindoo law and life at the
present day. Five or six centuries after the compo-

sition of this code the troops of Alexander crossed the Indus. The picture which the Greeks give us of society as they observed it, accords with that which we gain from the earlier native source; but, what is still more to the point, it also accords in essentials with what our own countrymen tell us of India now. With the advantages we possess from the actual occupation of the country, from being able to examine parts of it which the Greeks never visited, and from modern habits of critical investigation, we must see many things much more clearly than they did; and therefore, even when their reports are different from the present state of things, it is not necessary to assume that there must have been really a great change. It is hardly needful, however, to take this remark into consideration, for we are assured, by those who have the best opportunities of judging, that one of the most remarkable features of Hindoo life, the constitution and government of the villages, is exhibited with surprizing faithfulness in narratives which were derived from observations made more than 2000 years ago. Such permanence in social habits would surely lead us to expect something corresponding to it in the inward convictions of a people; and we are not left to conjecture. The soldiers of Alexander found a set of men whose great business was contemplation, who submitted to numerous privations and austerities that they might pursue it more effectually. The Brahmins they found were the leading class in the country; mili-

tary, agricultural, commercial occupations were all
subordinate to theirs—all society had, in fact,
organized itself in conformity with their ideas.
The Greek fancied they had less to do with civil
affairs, than we know, from their own code, that they
must have had. But the general conception which
he formed of the Brahmins was singularly accurate.
He called them Sophists, a name, which, in his own
country, often denoted mere sceptics; here it had
no such signification, but it implied that the Brahmins were not merely priests, such as were to be
seen elsewhere, that their first business was *study*,
and that the purely sacerdotal office was secondary
to this. As the accounts which the Greek writers
give of the objects of Hindoo worship are meagre,
and evidently distorted by the desire of finding
resemblances to their own mythology, we might
suppose that, for our purpose, we cannot learn much
from them. But I believe we shall find that their
report of the Brahmins is, in fact, the key to the
whole system; one which, if we use it rightly,
will enable us to discover its leading characteristics,
and to understand, however little we may be able
to trace, the varieties of form which it has assumed.

The name of Brahmin at once suggests that
of Brahm. The resemblance is no accidental one;
nor does it merely signify that the Brahmin is
the minister or priest of Brahm. The connection
is of a far more intimate and wonderful kind.
The learned man, the contemplative sage, aspires
to be one with him whom he adores—to lose his

own being in his. And what is this Being? He
is the Absolute Intelligence; the Essential Light.
Rest, Contemplation: this is his glory, his perfection. You will feel at once the direct opposition
between this idea and that of the Mahometan. I
bring it before you just at this point, that you
may see how much we may impose upon ourselves
by the word Monotheism, which is often used as
if it were common to these two faiths, at least,
in their origin; that you may see at the same
time in what sense it has been honestly and rightly
applied to Hindooism. Mahometanism began with
a Prophet, but we saw the Prophet soon merged
in the Khalif or Sovereign. This Sovereign was
the organ of a Mighty Will, which had called all
things into existence, and of whom all men are
servants. He fulfils his service in perpetual conflict; only in such conflict does his faith make its
meaning intelligible. There are no natural gradations of society, no hereditary ranks; all are merely
officers holding their position under the one Ruler.
The priest is an insignificant person. Strictly
speaking, there is no priesthood. The dervish or
learned man may be an important adviser of the
sovereign: in times of quiet he may promote learning, or become the head of a sect; but when he
is most regarded it is only as an interpreter of
the Divine Will. The first principle of Mahometanism would be violated if he aspired to be
himself divine. Here, on the contrary, the priest,
the student, the beholder is judge, lawgiver, every-

thing. The God is an Intelligence, not a Will—
himself a higher priest—a more glorious student—
a more perfect contemplator. You can scarcely
conceive a mandate issuing from such a being:
all things must flow from him as light from the
sun, or thoughts from a musing man. Such an
idea is ever implied in Hindooism; but it may
not have been frequently expressed, it may sometimes have been contradicted, in the earliest stage;
for the wrapt student, feeling it his highest calling
and privilege to meditate on an Absolute Being
in silence and awe, will have had such a practical
reason for not confounding him with the world
around, as no theoretical consistency could out-
weigh. It was far otherwise with the feeling of a
relation between the human worshipper and the object of his adoration. This feeling was not resisted,
but strengthened by his practical discipline. He
was taught that he was intended to rise into the
closest communion, nay, into actual identity with
the Divinity: to realize such a state was the effort
of his existence.

The Brahmin believed that there was in *man*
a capacity for such intercourse or absorption as this;
but surely not in all men. Some are merely animal:
there must be a race intended for this high converse, there must be a race excluded from it. One
would not say, however, that the highest sage is
the only man who is not merely animal. The
warrior must have something of the higher diviner
faculty; it may be cultivated and ripened in him.

Even the merchant, the traveller into other lands, must be more than a merely earthly creature. These orders of men should be kept apart from the lowest of all—the mere human animal, the Sudra. Yet the purely contemplative man should not be allowed too much intercourse even with these. He may educate them to be such men as they are meant to be, but he must keep himself and his race pure: this race must be carefully trained to be the model of humanity—to rise above humanity—by perpetual meditation on the unseen Brahm.

The so-called laws or institutes of the Hindoos are all designed for this purpose. They are, properly speaking, a system of education or discipline; a method of fitting the highest man for fulfilling his vocation, and all the others for preserving their proper relation to him. The idea of a separation between the twice-born man and the merely animal man, is the fundamental one; all the arrangements are for the purpose of giving effect to this idea—all other distinctions are secondary to it. The twice-born man must, by certain services or sacraments, the principal of which is reading the Vedas, maintain his relation to the unseen object. He must practise certain plans for lessening his dependence on mere material gratifications; he must cultivate rather the passive than the active qualities. In the progress of ages the two middle classes seem to have disappeared, or at least this is the prevailing Brahminical opinion. The system

has undergone other modifications, till at length,
in some places at least, it has so adapted itself
to the different pursuits and occupations of men,
as to offer an excuse for the European notion,
that it was invented in an early stage of society
by some legislator, who observed that labour must
be divided in order to be successful, and that
there is likely to be an hereditary aptitude for
particular professions or trades. Such a notion
seems to be refuted by the fact that, according to
the early arrangement of castes, there was no
accurate division of employments ; that persons of
the same order were allowed to perform many
which were unlike and incompatible. Nor does
another plausible hypothesis, that the Brahmins
were a conquering tribe and the Sudras a conquered one, seem to be more tenable. Those who
have the best opportunities for comparing them,
say that they can discover no such differences between them as would warrant the supposition of
their belonging to a different race, none greater
than are naturally produced by meaner occupations,
and a sense of degradation during a long course
of years. But the great objection to the opinion
is, that the Sudras are not in any sense slaves,
and never can have been such; the Greeks were
surprized to find all classes in India free citizens in
some sense, in however low a one. So that probably we cannot get much further than the religious principle as the basis of the distinction—
than the idea, I mean, that there is a tendency

in men to become purely animal, and that there
is a race of men in which this tendency is realized
and perpetuated; that there is in man that which
may be raised to fellowship with the Divine; and
that there is a race in whom this capacity is exhibited and transmitted.

In spite then of the fact, that there are in the
very earliest Hindoo Vedas prayers and hymns to
light and fire, and to many natural powers, nay,
though the liturgical part of them consists mainly
of such prayers, we may fully admit the assertion,
that the Brahmin is seeking after one Divine, unseen
object; that he is only asking these different creatures to tell him what that object is, and how
He is to be found; nay, that his aim in his whole
life and discipline is to purify himself from outward,
sensible things, that he may approach nearer to
this One Source of Illumination.

But then how can we explain the fact, that
men setting this end before them, looking upon
the most mysterious powers in the universe as at
best ladders to ascend to the highest region—
ladders which the wise men could generally, in
time, throw away—should have become so utterly
entangled in sensible, outward idolatry as the modern Hindoo seems to be? The explanation often
given, that the ordinary gods are but the gods of the
vulgar, that the learned man has altogether another
view of them, which he keeps to himself, is quite
unsatisfactory. For the point we want to ascertain
is this, how the Brahmin came to suppose that the

divers and manifold beings of whom the Hindoo
Pantheon consists, could be helps to the discovery
or the presentation of the One Being; how he
could possibly be induced to reverse the whole order
and object of his studies and discipline; to introduce variety, that he might suggest the idea of
unity; to bring in a host of visible forms, that
he might lead his disciples more certainly to that
which is beyond their senses. I do not deny the
possibility of such a scheme, but the origin and
the steps of it should be explained. If a modern
Brahmin confesses that he attaches no importance
to the things to which he seems to attach the
greatest, we may accept his testimony against
himself; still more willingly we may believe one
who says that he loves the simple faith which he
thinks has departed, and that he will spend his
life in efforts to restore it. But we cannot take
the witness of either respecting their fathers. The
process by which they arrived at one strange conclusion after another may have been as simple
and natural a one as that by which their traditions are discarded, or that by which they are traced
to a deliberate purpose of imposture.

And this, I believe, is actually the case. While
the Brahmin was learning, by various arts, to practise abstraction of spirit, was searching, by various
helps, to arrive at the perception of the Perfect
One, he felt that the light, the intelligence which
entered into his own heart—that which raised him
above his fellows—that which enabled him to see

mysteries, must be the great expression of the
Divine Being. Brahm becomes Brahma; the light
which flows from the source of light, the wisdom
which comes from the fount of wisdom is that which
declares him—this is his Name. In that character
the initiated disciple is to worship him: no sacrifices need be offered to him, no temples need be
raised to him. It is the inward and purified intellect which does him homage. A very sublime conception, you may be inclined to say; one which
it is no wonder that enlightened Brahmins in our
day should wish to reproduce.

But imagine yourselves in the school where
this sublime doctrine was taught; look at the
self-satisfied, self-glorified person who is proclaiming it; see how he has gone on, step by step, till,
from a profound idea of some awful, absolute
Being, he has passed into the habitual conviction
that this Being is himself; he has become his
own God. Mark what contempt he manifests
for persons about him, what utter inhumanity
has grown out of this notion, that he is the
very perfection of humanity, that he is above it.
Suppose an earnest, enthusiastic disciple, struck
with the contradiction, saying to himself, " Is this
the devout, the self-losing, absorbed Brahmin whom
I was taught to wonder at—whose teaching at first
seemed to me so sublime?" In the tumult of his
feelings, in the sadness of his disappointment, he
goes forth from the school into Nature. What a
change he finds there! What a sense of refresh-

ment, freedom, calmness, penetrates through his
whole being! Surely he has been living till this
time in a close, pent-up atmosphere, thinking only
of himself; ever hoping, and hoping in vain, to
find his God in himself. But is he not here?
What a wonderful order there is through this
wide universe; an order of day and night; of seasons of heat and seasons of rain; an order in the
planets over our heads; an order in the growth
of the flowers at our feet; an order in the over-
flowings of the mighty river. Yes, his name is the
Preserver! Conceive of him under that name—
worship him under that name—call him Vishnu:
bid men rejoice that they have such an One caring
for them. The name, perhaps, had been known
before in the Brahminical school. It had been one
thought, among many, that Brahma was the preserver of things: now it becomes THE name. Hun-
dreds of hearts are ready to welcome it : even the
poor Sudra can look up, and feel that it has a
sound of blessing to him. And now the older
worship becomes, comparatively, obsolete; the young
reformer has prevailed. The Brahminical order must
take up his doctrine, and proclaim it, and reconcile it as they can with that which they held
before: if they do not so, a sect of Vishnu worshippers will form themselves—men will go out
into the deserts and proclaim this faith, without
respect to the laws of family or caste at all.

In some such way as this, I conceive, the popular
Vishnu worship may have supplanted the original

Brahma worship. It would be surely hard to say
that the alteration was in itself for the worse:
yet the effect of it must, undoubtedly, have been
to withdraw the idea of divinity from the inner
sanctuary in which it had dwelt; to bring it forth
into the world. Then 'temples would be raised,
the fruits of the earth offered, with songs and
symbols, to the great Preserver. But soon there
will have been a fearful re-action against this kind
of service. How could the mere feeling of a beneficent Guardian of the Earth help men who were
tormented with a sense of inward evil? What was
there in such a Being at all corresponding to the
dark visions which continually rose before them,
whether they looked behind or before, to the past
or the future. But was there nothing in Nature
which did correspond to these inward agonies,
which seemed to be the very echo of them? Were
there no frightful floods and earthquakes—was there
not a continual process of destruction going on in
the universe? Is not death the mighty king to
whom all must do homage? Poor worshippers of
Vishnu, how miserably you are striving to hide
the realities of the world from your eyes—to strew
garlands over the grave. You have never yet dared
to pronounce the real name: it is Sheeva the Destroyer. If you know your own state, and what
you have to fear, you will invoke that name—you
will propitiate that divinity. And do not think
to approach him with such oblations as are signs
of plenty and gladness. It is blood he craves for;

the blood of your children and of yourselves. No
sacrifices but these can appease his wrath, or abate
the misery which he is sending to you, and de-
signing for you. Here was another deep conviction working in the heart of the Hindoo, and destined to produce the most fearful fruits, from generation to generation. The Brahmins could not allay
it—could not reduce it under his old notion of
the Brahma, the one celestial Intelligence, who
spoke only in the Wise. The Sheeva sect rose
up in fierce antagonism to the Vishnu sect. He
must endeavour to bring the different ideas into
reconciliation; to assign the Brahma, the Vishnu,
and Sheeva, each a part in the arrangements of
Nature, and in the different ages of the universe.
Religious books are composed, some with the Vishnu, some with the Sheeva element predominant
in them; the former with a gracious, the latter
with a stern, forbidding aspect; the first not
denying the dark principle—only keeping it in
the back-ground; the latter doing homage to the
Preserver, but confessing the greater might of the
Destroyer.

Soon the unsatisfied heart feels another necessity. If it be true (and can it be denied?)
that the Power which divides and annihilates has
such a direct influence over the destinies of the
world, may not the Preserver yet have somewhere
an undisturbed reign; and may he not descend
from that region, at certain periods, to claim his
rights over this earth too—to create again that

which has perished? Is there not a principle of
restoration implied in Preservation; nay, in Destruction itself? The animals die, but the race
survives: and have there not been in the ages of
man periods of deepest calamity, when all things
seemed to sink in utter ruin, followed by bright
sunny days—the earth coming forth out of darkness into light? These must have been the times
of Vishnu's descent. These animals, we have been
told, all exhibit some side or aspect of the divinity,
may have been, originally, portions of it. In these
he may have appeared. Men may have been able,
without becoming absorbed, to behold him, and
converse with him. Again, the priest will partly
have led the popular conviction, partly have been
led by it. He will have arranged the number
and method of these Vishnu incarnations, reducing
dreams to a system, and sanctioning the hope that
there might be an avater, which should restore
all things.

But these dreams were not sufficient. Was
not a kind and gracious Rajah, who felt for his
poor subjects, one in whom the Divinity was more
likely to manifest himself, than in any one of those
creatures, however sacred, of which man is practically the master? Have we not always felt that
a man was permitted, in some mysterious way, to
contemplate the Divine Being—to become one
with Him? Why may not He in such a form,
so much more beautiful than any other, appear
to us? The bright Krishna becomes the centre of

innumerable legends. He is felt to be the true
form of the Divine Deliverer. As other dreadful
apparitions rise up beside Sheeva, and claim the
kind of worship which is offered to him—as there
comes forth even a Kali to be a patroness of
murder, to make strangling a virtue; this image
of a friend and protector of the helpless is the more
eagerly sought after, and delighted in.

At each step in this process more of the forms
and images of outward nature will have been called
in, to express the conception of which the heart
was full; at each step the theoretic man will have
been obliged to incorporate new schemes of the
universe, new speculations upon all questions —
astronomical, geological, physiological, metaphysical, into his theology, in order to connect the
later and more popular outgrowths of it with the
original root. Nevertheless, it is certain that,
amidst all these definite conceptions and idolatrous
forms, the primary idea of an Inconceivable, Absolute, Unseen Being, whom it is the highest glory
of the holiest man to behold, and in whom he
is to be lost, has survived—survived not as a theory
of some learned Brahmin, but as so deep and essential an article of popular faith, that all other
habitual convictions, nay, the reverence for the
Brahminical order itself, which seems worked into
the very tissue of Hindoo society, must give place
to it. Religious orders, formed without any reference to distinction of castes, shall be followed and
reverenced in proportion as this seems to be the

end of their existence: the perfectly abstracted
Yogi shall be looked upon as greater, in the way
to a higher knowledge, than he who can explain
all the order of nature. In fact, in the worst form
of what may be supposed modern corruptions we
may trace the original feeling at work. The woman
who gives up herself to death on her husband's
funeral pile, is exhibiting the same deep sense
of the necessity of self-abandonment, self-sacrifice,
which is implied in the desire of the contemplative
man to be absorbed into the Divine Essence.

We have, then, a faith presented to us here,
which the more we think of it, the more fairly we
consider its apparent anomalies, the more light
we receive respecting it from different and contradictory reports, the more heartily and affec-
tionately we sympathize with the feelings of our
fellow-men, the more we know of ourselves, will
awaken in us the more of reflection, and wonder,
and awe. It is the faith not of savages but of
men in whose minds respect for learning has occupied all but the highest place; men whose whole
commonwealth is modelled upon the notion, that
the seer, the learned man, ought to be at the
head; that all other people should look up to him.
At the same time, these learned men have not
been able to devise a belief at their pleasure for
those whom they governed. Strong necessities have
come forth out of the heart of the people, de-
manding satisfaction—compelling the wise men to
remould their system, yet recognizing the worth

and reality of that higher, older principle, which they seem to set at nought. I do not think it would be easy to find a fairer test of those assertions, respecting the religions of mankind, which I proposed to examine.

The first of them—that there are deep truths implied in each of these systems—receives, it seems to me, abundant confirmation from even the hasty glance we have been able to take of Hindooism. In the midst of the extravagancies and horrors which the most favourable testimonies prove it to have brought forth, and which have multiplied, not diminished, as it has expanded, we have been able to trace some convictions so sacred, so bound up in the heart of the people for thousands of years, as to sustain the credit of monstrous fictions, to make tormenting practices endurable; convictions which have been able to create and perpetuate a complicated form of society, and to defy the power of victorious invaders.

But it is affirmed next, that these deep convictions will in time disengage themselves, from the theological element in which they dwell; that theology being only an inadequate attempt to explain the phenomena of the universe. Now, I have been careful that you should notice how much of the Hindoo system *is* an attempt to explain the phenomena of the universe; it was scarcely necessary for me to remark how ineffectual a one. But, if you have followed the course of my observations, still more, if you have made observations for yourselves, you will, I think, be convinced that these theories about the world are precisely the non-theological element of the system; precisely that which has been added to the theology, and become a part of it, in consequence of the inability of the Hindoo to distinguish between God and the world. His inward convictions, from first to last, have had reference to the Absolute, Unseen God, and to his relations with man. The drapery of these convictions has been his doctrine about Nature. Nor can that idolatrous, degrading, often filthy drapery ever be cast away, unless it can be shewn him that the theological riddles, for which he has been seeking a solution in Nature so long, and not finding it—which are bound up with the deepest wants of his heart, can receive their explanation somewhere else.

But, most of all, the notion that all ideas respecting an unseen world are produced by the religious faculty in man, might seem to receive countenance from the Hindoo records. How active that faculty has been, what worlds it has called into existence, whilst there were no outward transactions to relate, or no one to relate them, we have indeed seen. The Hindoo in action the idlest, is in imagining, dreaming, combining, the most busy of all human creatures. But is this all we have learnt? Have we not found also an assurance in the mind of these people that all the efforts of thought in them must originate in a communication from above, and require fresh

communications to meet them ?   In the thinking,
or reasoning, or religious faculty, call it what you
will—or, as I should say, in the man's own
heart, in his inmost being—have arisen desires,
and longings after converse with the unseen world,
with some living being in that unseen world,
with some one between whom and himself he feels
there is a relation.   His religious books echo the
cry; they mutter a half response to it: but the
response is only the question thrown into a more
definite form.   The highest student meditates on
the problem, and repeats his own thoughts; or,
more probably, what some ancient person, who meditated and conversed with the Divinity, said about
it; or what some other said that he said.   The
circle is a very weary one ; if we calmly consider
it, and what kind of comfort those receive who
are ever revolving in it, we shall confess that the
Hindoo is right in his belief, that the wisdom of
which he sees the image and reflection must
speak and declare itself to him; that he cannot
always be left to grope his way amidst the shadows
which it casts in his own mind, or in the world
around him.   I ask nothing more than the Hindoo
system and the Hindoo life as evidence that there
is that in man which demands a revelation—that
there is not that in him which makes the revelation.   I ask no clearer proof of the fact, that whenever the religious feeling or instinct in man works
freely, without an historical revelation, it must

beget a system of priestcraft. It must be satisfied
by God, or overlaid by man, or stifled altogether.

The question still remains: Is the help to this
state of things to come from within the system?
I hinted that there are, or have been, Hindoo
patriots who have dreamed of bringing back the
first state of Brahminism, setting up the Monotheism of the older Vedas, sweeping away the
accumulations of centuries. But if the original
Brahminism itself contained the great puzzle of
all subsequent ages; if the Monotheism of the
Vedas admitted the doubt whether man, nay,
whether all things might not be parts of the
Divinity; if those accumulations of centuries were
the inevitable results of anxieties which men could
only quell by destroying themselves, it seems somewhat unreasonable to go back to the beginning
of a series, every step of which, so far as we can tell,
would have to be repeated. Or, if the notion be,
that some form of Monotheism, not involving the
idea of direct connection between God and Man,
or God and Nature, might supersede the existing
superstition, is it not playing with words to speak
of this as a revival or restoration? must it not
be simply a denial of the fundamental principle
of the whole system? We need not, however, enter
upon this subject at present, for both these ex-
periments have been made under every possible
advantage. Buddhism, a doctrine to which I
hope to devote a separate Lecture, may, at least

under one of its aspects, be regarded as a formal
effort to revive the original Brahminical idea ; an
effort not without very important results, which
have affected a large portion of the world ; but
which have not displaced Hindooism in its proper
soil, and which, I think, we shall find are scarcely
what any modern Hindoo reformer would desire
to produce. To the other experiment I have
alluded already—it is that of Mahometanism. A
considerable number of the Hindoo race were converted to this faith, and profess it to this day.
But it could take no hold of the heart of the
people, for it solved no one difficulty which was
perplexing them; it affirmed a truth which stag-
gered them, and before which they bowed ; one, however, which in this form coalesced with scarcely any
conditions of their intellectual or of their moral being.

Whether Christianity can do for the Hindoo
what these systems have not done, is a question for
our future consideration. One or two remarks I
would make here which may remove some difficulties from that enquiry, and which seem to
arise naturally out of the present subject. I cannot feel surprize that the statesmen and scholars
of British India, observing the failure of the Mahometans to overthrow the faith and institutions
of this strange people, should have pressed strongly
upon their own government the duty of respecting
what it had not power to subvert. I cannot believe
that an indifference to evils which were continually

before their eyes, or a feeling that the safety of English dominion is the highest of all considerations, can
have induced men often of the greatest cultivation
and humanity to protest against the efforts which
some of their countrymen were making to spread the
faith of Europe in the East. It is much pleasanter,
and surely more reasonable, to believe that they felt
there was something hard-hearted, almost impious,
in trampling upon convictions which had struck
root into the soil for many thousand years, which
had created the whole fabric of society. For such
a feeling one is bound to entertain the greatest
respect; only I think men generally so clear-sighted
must by this time have perceived that there was
an important oversight in the inference which they
drew from it. No doubt it is a very serious thing
to assault the belief, even the prejudices, of any
ancient people. But this assault had already been
made; every circumstance which brought Englishmen into contact with the Hindoo was a repetition
of it. When all nature is peopled with divinities
it does not require an adverse theologian to wound
the prejudices of the worshipper,—the army com-
missary, the judge, the ordinary traveller, must
interfere with them continually. Above all, when
it came to be perceived, as it would of course be
in time perceived by any benevolent government,
that Englishmen ought not to be settled in a
country without communicating to its inhabitants
some portion of that knowledge which they possess

so largely; or rather, when it was found that a
people so eager for information, so quick in re-
ceiving it as the Hindoos, would not be content
until they had learnt the secret of our mechanical
achievements,—it was certain that some cherished
tenet must be outraged, some express statement
in the religious books contradicted, if the teacher
of European science advanced beyond his alphabet.
Such considerations do not prove that the idea
of respecting a people's convictions is a false one;
they show only that there are certain accidents
of these convictions which we are not only permitted, but obliged, to make light of. Just in
proportion to that necessity which is laid upon
us for showing the Hindoo that visible things
cannot be treated with the reverence which he
has been taught to feel for them, should be our
desire and determination to preserve him from the
danger to which he is certainly exposed, of thinking
that all the questionings of his fathers respecting
the invisible world had no purpose or meaning.
These questionings belong to the most radical
portion of the Hindoo mind; in them you see
what the Hindoo is, what his existence means,
and how he has been able to stamp such an image
of himself upon society. To these questionings he
owes the activity of his intellect and imagination
when all his other tendencies and his outward
circumstances would make him indolent—hence have
arisen his love of letters and his desire for science.
But the time has evidently come when he cannot

be questioning merely; he must have answers. I
contend that he who is able to give them is not
a destroyer, but a preserver; that he will have a
right to boast of having upheld all that was
strongest and most permanent in the Hindoo life and
character, while other influences, however innocently
and inevitably, were threatening to undermine them.
I concede with equal readiness, that if Christianity
do not offer these answers, it cannot make this
boast; it must leave to some other instrument the
work of regenerating Hindostan. As the question
is brought to this test, let us gather up in a few
words the enigmas which have tormented the Hindoo so long, and of which, for the sake of his
practical life, he demands a solution.

First, he has had the deepest assurance that
God must be an Absolute and Living Being, who
can be satisfied with nothing less perfect than
himself; and yet he has an equally deep conviction
that this Absolute and Eternal Being cannot
merely live in self-contemplation; that there must
be some object in which He sees His image reflected. The thought is expressed with great earnestness and beauty in one of the early Vedas,
where Brahm is introduced seeking for the image
of himself. The words which are imputed to him
express the strong feeling, that a merely solitary,
self-seeking, abstracted being would be one whom
a man, experiencing his own need of sympathy and
fellowship, could not bear to contemplate. The
thought expands itself through the whole Hindoo

mythology. It utters itself from the beginning
in the idea of a Brahma, as well as a Brahm; it
gives birth to all the later notions of goddesses
dwelling beside the gods. If no voice comes from
the secret place to interpret this mighty contradiction which the learned man has perceived, which
the most ignorant Hindoo feels, their thoughts of
God and their human life must continue a hopeless
maze.

For the perplexity which grows out of this
lies close to personal, as well as social existence.
May not man himself be this partner of the Divinity? If he is, what means that deep assurance
of a Divinity retired within the sanctity and awful-
ness of his own nature?—if he is not, what mean
these yearnings in the spirit after the knowledge
of him; this promise in the heart that it may be
attained; this discontent while it is wanting? It
is an idle thing to cut this knot by affirming
either principle and denying the other; all confusions, theoretical and practical, of the Hindoo
arise from the attempt to do this, and from the
experience of its impossibility; only if you can
shew that they have been reconciled, and how,
will you lead him to any clearness or freedom. Man
has this glorious faculty; but a portion of men
seem without it. It must dwell in a caste; the
rest must be cut off from it. Leave this thought
to work, and it will bring forth the fruits which
it has brought forth hitherto. The modern Hindoo, with his European culture and science, will

be just as contemptuous to all who want his information and intellect as the Brahmins of old;
the twice-born notion may change its form, in
effect it will be as rampant and tyrannical as ever.
You cannot extirpate it, until you justify it —
until you can shew that some eternal truth lies in
the distinction, and yet that it excludes no human
creature; that it asserts the common privilege of
Brahmin and Sudra.

Then we come to another set of questions—
This Absolute Being, what manner of being is
he? If it be true that he stands in some relation
to us and the world, in what relation? Is he
benignant, or hateful? is he a preserver or destroyer?
You cannot answer the question with any vague
flourishes of rhetoric. The Hindoo is willing
enough to acknowledge a kind and gracious ruler,
but the worshipper of Sheeva meets you with a
set of facts. Here is misery, here is death. You
must encounter these facts—you cannot blink them.
You must be able to say—"I can shew that this
misery and death do not interfere with the idea
of a God of Order, Mercy, Love; I can shew it
by practical tokens and demonstrations;" otherwise
you must leave the sects to fight on for ever,
with a tolerable certainty that the darker will in
general have the ascendency. Again, the idea of
a struggle between life and death, order and disorder, good and evil, and of the victory having
been achieved by the God actually descending into
the battle-field, and himself taking part in the

strife; the idea that he must assume some form
which is subject to all the accidents of earthly
calamity; this is one which a European may easily
scoff at, when he sees it presented to him in the
Hindoo stories, and, doubtless, he will find many
a learned Brahmin who is ready, with more or
less reserve, to scoff too, nay, to represent such a
notion as quite incompatible with the higher Brahminical theology. But let it be well considered
that a stern demand of the popular conscience
carries with it a very mighty witness; if the
learned order bows to that demand, allows the
people to clothe their inward belief in their own
shapes, and reduces their crudities to a system,
we may be sure that the faith of the taught is
stronger and more vital than that of the teacher;
it may be grosser, but it must contain, at least,
as real an element. Except this part of the Hindoo
conviction can be recognized; unless it can be shewn
how the belief of such a divine descent is compatible with the highest idea any Brahmin can
entertain of the divine perfection, or of man's spirit
being intended to ascend to the apprehension and
participation of it; I cannot see how the Hindoo
race can ever be permanently raised above its present degradation, or how that respect and justice,
which have been so passionately demanded for the
faith and institutions of centuries, can be practically rendered. Once more—It is, undoubtedly,
a right thing in a government to suppress, by actual
edict and physical force, human sacrifices. The

Roman, tolerant as he was of all polytheistic systems in the provinces, took this course in our
own country when he was dealing with the practices
of Druidical worship. But neither by this act, nor
by establishing municipal institutions in Britain,
nor by building and encouraging the natives to build
baths, and porticoes, and temples, did he provide
any real substitute for those dark, mysterious
thoughts of the unseen world, which had haunted
the mind of the Celt under his oaks, and which
found a fearful expression in these sacrifices. Those
thoughts were the stamina of the British heart;
when an external civilization expelled them, what
remained was a feeble colony, groaning for help
to the masters who could give it help no longer;
a colony which needed to have all its arts and
polish destroyed by a people possessing some real
faith, some inward strength, that the soil might,
by this process, be prepared to bear genuine native
fruits. It will be the same with Hindostan, if,
while we put down the burnings of widows, and
bestow a culture which makes such practices dis-
gusting, we are not able to shew them what is
the true form of self-immolation, and how wife, and
maiden, and widow—how men, whether called to
the contemplative, or active life, may practise it.

I know that I am asking no light thing of any
faith when I say, All this it must do if it is
to satisfy the heart and conscience of this Asiatic
people. But let me ask you, before I conclude,
whether a faith which does less than this can satisfy

your hearts and consciences? We are in a world
of action, and energy, and enterprize, more unlike
that dreaming and speculative world we have been
hearing of than the soil and climate of England
are unlike those of Hindostan. And yet, I will
be bold to say it, the same thoughts which stir
the spirit of the Indian sage and the Indian
Sudra, are working secretly beneath all our bus-
tling life, are affecting the councils of statesmen,
are entering into the meditations of the moralists
and metaphysicians who most despise theology;
in another form, are disturbing the heart of the
country peasant, and the dweller in St. Giles's.
They are such questions as these—What do we
worship? A dream, or a real Being? One wholly
removed from us, or one related to us? Is He a
Preserver, or a Destroyer? Has Death explained
its meaning to us, or is it still a horrible riddle?
Is it still uncertain whether Life or Death is master
of the world, or how has the uncertainty been removed? What is the evil which I find in myself?
Is it myself? Must *I* perish in order that it may
perish, or can it be in any wise separated from
me? Can I give up myself, and yet live? What
are these desires which I feel in myself for something unseen, glorious, and perfect? Are they all
phantasy, or can they be realized? If they can, by
what means? Has He to whom they point made
himself known to me? How am I connected with
Him? Must I utterly renounce all the things about
me, that I may be absorbed into Him, or is there any

way in which I can devote them and myself to Him, and only know Him the better by fulfilling my place among them? These are the great human questions; distance in time and space does not affect them; if we are not concerned with them, it is because we have not yet ceased to be savages, or because we are returning, through an extreme civilization, into the state of savages: if they do occupy us, we shall find that there can be but one answer to them for the Englishman and the Hindoo.

LECTURE III.

In my former Lectures I have spoken of two religions, very opposite in their character, which have exercised an influence over a large portion of the world—the Mahometan and the Hindoo. The former, we said, could only thrive when it was in action; the proper element of the other was rest. They were brought face to face in Hindostan. The Islamite triumphed, as might have been expected; but there was a passive strength in the Hindoo, which ultimately kept its ground, and enables him to say that his system has endured for 3000 years.

I hinted that it had had struggles with a very different kind of enemy from the Mahometan—with a doctrine in many of its essential peculiarities like its own. That doctrine is the Buddhist, the faith of Thibet, of Siam, of the Burmese Empire, of Cochin China, Japan, Ceylon; the popular, though not the state, faith of China. It is said to number above 300 millions of people among its disciples; to be, therefore, by far the most prevailing religion which does exist, or ever has existed, in the world. It is, surely then, deserving of earnest investigation; there must be something in it which has given it this wide diffusion. It must express some

5—2

necessities of man's heart, some necessities of our own.

I propose, in the present Lecture, to enquire what these are; to search for the main principle of Buddhism; to consider in what relation it stands to those religions of which we have spoken ; lastly, how it is connected with two other systems which divide with it the Celestial Empire.

A faith which is spread over such a number of countries, many of them very different from each other in outward circumstances, perhaps even in race and early cultivation, must present great varieties, which may seem to make the use of a common name rather a convenient refuge for our ignorance, than a proof that they have really any connection. Undoubtedly our information respecting the different forms of Buddhism is still very imperfect, and we have not the same means of correcting and enlarging it, as in the case of countries which have fallen under our own dominion. Ceylon is, I believe, the only British possession in which pure Buddhism is professed. Nevertheless, I am convinced that the intelligent travellers and residents who have given us accounts of what they have seen or heard in the different countries I have enumerated, or of what they have read in the books which these countries account sacred, have not been mistaken in believing that the fundamental doctrine is the same in all. The opposition between different views of the system, great as it is, admits, I think, of a tolerably easy

explanation; easy, at least, if we do not merely
look to find a meaning in the dry records of other
people's notions or practices, but compare them
with what we have felt and experienced in our own
lives. The numerous phases, however, which the
system assumes, make it very desirable that we
should ascertain from what country it was derived,
where we may seek for the first form of it. On
this subject there is some, but, I think, now not
much, difference of opinion. The external arguments which induced Sir William Jones, and some
eminent scholars of the last century, to suppose that
its native seat could not have been Hindostan, have
given way to later and fuller information. There
was a stronger internal argument, arising from a
comparison of the Brahminical and Buddhist faith,
which is also, it seems to me, untenable; but which
is well worth considering, and which at once connects the present subject with that of the last
Lecture.

We do not adequately describe the condition
of Hindostan, by saying that the priests constitute its leading caste. The whole form of society has a sacerdotal stamp upon it; it has
moulded itself in conformity with a religious idea;
not, as some have fancied, with a professional or
mercantile one. And yet, when we look into the
meaning of this system it explains itself, by the
doctrine that there is in *man* a capacity for be-
holding the Unseen Being, and that there is in
man an animal nature which admits of no Divine

converse. The Brahmin is the learned, divine, absorbed man, the end of whose existence is to become one with Brahm.

Brahm himself, I observed, was emphatically an Intelligence, a thinking, not a commanding being —One from whose thoughts all the universe has flowed out, not one by whose will it has been created. He is a higher priest, not in any sense a sovereign; herein standing in the most direct contrast to the object of Mahometan worship. Between, then, the god and the worshipper there is the most direct affinity, which may become identity. Intelligence is to be the characteristic of both. The hereditary caste is to preserve this Intelligence; its discipline to prevent it from being debased by mixture with people in whom the lower nature is predominant, or by contact with things which may make it predominant in themselves.

Now that any set of men should arise in a society, constituted like that of Hindostan, to deny the existence of a special caste of priests, might not seem surprising; for one might conjecture that there would be popular re-actions against so very strict and exclusive a system. We saw that there had been such popular re-actions in Hindostan. They took this form. They demanded a being less abstract than Brahm; not a mere thinking being, but one who should exercise actual influence over the arrangements of Nature and the world— one to whom its good or its evil might be ascribed— one who should not merely cultivate intercourse

with an absorbed devotee, but should enter into
fellowship with human creatures in their ordinary
condition. To such strong workings of popular
feeling, to such cries of the popular heart, we
traced the Vishnu and Sheeva worship, which the
priests had been compelled to incorporate with that
older principle it seemed striving to subvert. It
is evident that in these cases the priestly caste,
whatever rude shocks it may have sustained, nevertheless kept its ground, even in the hearts of the
people who assailed it. In fact, nothing proves
more clearly than such changes, how much the
reverence for a priestly order has been bound up
with the sympathies and character of this nation.
Neither the awakening of impulses which the
priests could not control, nor conquest by such an
utterly unsacerdotal people as the Mahometans,
have availed to weaken this reverence. The priests
have adapted themselves to feelings which they
could not subdue: their authority has waxed
stronger by a doctrine which threatened to crush
it and the popular faith together.

But the Buddhist doctrine cannot in any wise
be identified with this kind of movement. The
word Buddha, it seems to be admitted on all hands,
means Intelligence. That men ought to worship
pure Intelligence, must have been the first proclamation of the original Buddhists. The deduc-
tion from this must have been, that no caste of
priests was necessary for such worship. Could this
doctrine have originated on the soil of Hindostan?

I do not wonder that thoughtful persons, especially those whose experience made them aware of the facts I have just alluded to, should have said that it could not : that a theory so contrary to the tendencies of Hindoos from generation to generation, must have come from some other region, and been rudely forced for a time upon this. But, plausible as such an hypothesis may seem, I think I have given you sufficient reason for distrusting it. The sacerdotal principle has indeed struck its roots very deep into the Indian soil, probably from as early a time as any to which we can possibly look back. It has shewn itself to be, in some form or other, inseparable from that soil. But it has grown up side by side with another principle, from which, at times, it is hardly distinguishable; the reverence for human intelligence; the disposition to make this the great Brahminical characteristic. It is quite conceivable, then, that from a very early time two sets of men may have co-existed in Hindostan; one composing an hereditary order of priests, the other a mere order of sages or devotees. They co-exist in India to the present day, on terms not probably of sympathy, but also not of absolute opposition or repulsion. The Greek writers allude to two classes seen by the soldiers of Alexander, between whom it has been reasonably enough supposed that a relation similar to this may have subsisted.

Both will alike have aimed at converse with the pure Intelligence, absorption into him. Both

therefore will have been far removed from any wish
to substitute for this object of worship one of a
more visible and earthly character.   But different
circumstances may have operated to draw each of
them into closer connection with that which is
visible.   The hereditary priest will have maintained
his position by taking part in civil employments—
will gradually have exhibited less of the higher
and more abstracted character.   The devotee will
have been reverenced by the people for retaining
and carrying out this character.   Thus he will
have been brought into greater sympathy with
them; will have been induced to symbolize the
object of his worship, that it might be more
apparent to ordinary men.   In this way, perhaps,
we may account for the appearance of temples,
possessing the characteristics of Buddhism, which
must have existed in Hindostan from a very early
period.   Gradually the distinction between these
classes will have become more marked and definite.
Sages will have appeared calling upon men to
adore Buddha in purity and simplicity, denouncing
the hereditary caste, denouncing the books upon
which they rested their pretensions, acknowledging a modified sympathy with the worship of the
people, as opposed to that of the Brahmins.   In
what light these sages were regarded we shall consider hereafter; now it is only necessary to observe
that there are the widest differences of opinion
among Buddhists respecting the time in which the
original sage, the first Buddhist teacher, flourished.

That one Sakya Muni appeared in the sixth century before Christ, who produced an effect upon
the inhabitants of India of the kind I have just
described, and that he left a series of successors,
seems to be ascertained. But he was in all pro-
bability only the rekindler of feelings, which had
been existing previously; only the person who
formally set them in opposition to the Brahminical
tendencies with which they had been hitherto,
though by somewhat loose and fragile links, associated. Although, then, I would by no means
support a paradox which has had some countenance
from learned men, but not from the most learned or
those who have examined the subject most, that
Buddhism was the original doctrine, of which Brahminism was a depravation—though such an opinion
has to struggle with the greatest opposition of
outward facts, and is, I think, also quite inconsistent with the respective character of the two
systems; yet I imagine we must look upon Hindostan as the place from which both have started,
must assume that they were branches from the
same root, and that their separation, however decided at last, was a slow and gradual work. Ultimately the systems did come into direct collision,
and it became evident that they could not dwell together on the same soil. The Brahminical succeeded
in expelling its rival from Hindostan, and it went
forth to seek and to find an asylum first in one,
then in another of those numerous Asiatic countries
which it now claims as its own.

This view of the origin of Buddhism may be
a great help, I think, in reconciling the very opposite
reports of it which we obtain from those who have
seen it in different, or even in the same localities.
The extreme Polytheism of India we found was not
so incompatible with what was said of its original
Monotheism, as it appeared at first   But what are
we to say of a doctrine which is sometimes represented as one of almost perfect Theism; sometimes as direct Atheism; sometimes as having the
closest analogy to what in a Greek philosopher, or
in a modern philosopher, would be called Pantheism;
sometimes as the worship of human saints or
heroes; sometimes as altogether symbolical; sometimes as full of the highest abstract speculation;
sometimes as vulgar idolatry? Strange as it may
seem, the same doctrine is, I believe, capable of
assuming all these different phases; no one of them
can be thoroughly understood without reference to
the other. Each is very imperfectly denoted by
the names which I have used; for the feelings,
good and evil, which work in the hearts of human
beings, can never be satisfactorily expressed by mere
labels describing a notion or theory.

I.   Thus, to begin with the first supposition.
Buddhism is, as we have seen, an attempt at the
highest, least material idea of divinity.   Buddha is
clear light, perfect wisdom.   You must not try to
conceive of him as doing anything.   Rest is not so
much his attribute, as his very essence.   He is One,
the One; and it is only with the inward eye,

purged from sensual corruptions, and steadily fixed
on the contemplation of unity, that he can in any
wise be apprehended. For the natural eye of the
ordinary man views a multiplicity of things, each
thing divided and separate from the other. The
natural eye takes account only of appearances;
it requires the severest discipline for a man to
behold the Reality. This is surely Theism in its
highest form and conception. It is something much
more than we are wont to mean by that word, for
by a Deist or Theist we often describe a person
who does not deny the existence of God; who
admits it as a sort of ultimate fact, as the Hercules'
pillar of the universe. But to the Buddhist, the
belief in God is the most awful, and at the same
time the most real of all thoughts; one not thrust
back into the corner of a mind which is occupied by
everything else, but which he thinks demands the
highest and most refined exercise of all the faculty
that he has. It is something which is to make
a change in himself, which is at once to destroy
him and to perfect him. And the effect is a practical one. Buddha is ever at rest. Can his worshippers be turbulent? Can he admit any rude
or violent passions into his heart? He must cultivate gentleness, evenness, all serene and peaceful
qualities, reverence and tenderness to all creatures,
or he is not in his rightful state. He is not tempted, or obliged, as the Brahmin is, to look upon any
human creature as merely animal, as excluded
even from the highest privileges. He denies the

natural difference of the Sudra; the poorest men
of the vilest race may become one with Buddha.
Hence, though he belongs to no priestly family,
all his functions are more essentially those of a
priest than the Brahmin's can be. He claims no
civil distinction; he is to be reverenced simply as
offering up prayers for the peace and prosperity
of all other people. He must abstain from much
speech. In silence he may best hope to know the
Unseen Intelligence. This is one aspect of the
doctrine, and surely a very interesting one.

II. But if the Buddist sage asks himself, What
is it that I am contemplating: I cannot see it, or
hear it, or handle it; I dare not conceive it; it is
altogether inconceivable, and yet I know of it only
by this mind of mine: he is likely to find himself
in a strange perplexity. Or, if he put the case thus
to himself: The end I propose to myself is to become nothing. Can it be Something which is to
work this result? Can it be Something I am contemplating? He must say at length, No, it is Nothing. Nothing must be the ground of my life, of
my being—of the being of all the things I see!
Here is Atheism; a deep, hopeless void, yet touch-
ing on the borders of that doctrine which implied
real belief in a living Divinity.

The transition to such Atheism is, no doubt,
possible in the Brahminical doctrine; but here it
is much easier. For the existence of a continuous
caste preserves the tradition of a Divinity, invests
it with a reality in some sense independent of the

mind of the beholder. Here all rests upon that
mind. The light seems to be projected from the
eye; now it may be a bright sun in the heaven;
now it may shrink into a speck; now it may
vanish altogether. Yet we should draw a wrong
inference from the incapacity of the Buddhist in this
state of mind to give any form to his belief, if we
said that it is wanting. He may even declare in honesty, 'I see nothing,' and the words being the
utterance of despair, not of triumph or satisfaction,
may themselves contain a sure witness, even to
himself, that there is that which no words or
thoughts of his can comprehend; an eternal absolute ground of all words and thoughts.

III. And soon the Buddhist discovers an escape
from this void of nothingness. He began with looking upon the One Intelligence as alone real; all outward nature he discarded, as merely apparent. But
the visible world claims its rights; he cannot
disown it; he must, in some way or other, take
it into his system. The Intelligence therefore, the
pure Buddha, must have a partner of his throne.
It is Dharma; the principle of Matter; that out
of which all things are formed. But these two
powers, Intelligence and Matter, seem essentially
opposite: if they are co-workers how can they be
reconciled? There must be another power, Sanga,
the mediating influence, which binds the informing
mind to the dead formless thing upon which it
works. This is nearly the explanation which a Buddhist priest gave to the English resident at Nepaul of

a subject which has occasioned much controversy. It is borne out by the symbols in the Buddhist temples. They seem contrived to express the idea of some active, productive power; of some passive, merely receptive power; again, of something which is the joint result of both. If we compare the Buddhist Triad with the Hindoo Triad of Brahma, Vishnu, and Sheeva, the Creator, Preserver, Destroyer, we are struck rather by their difference than their resemblance. The powers of preservation and destruction are militant powers; each is continually invading the kingdom of the other: Brahma is looked upon as the common origin of both. Here the Intelligent Power is considered as balancing, or sustaining, the Passive, Material Power; and a third as necessary to their fellowship. The latter idea is, I think, by far the deeper, and more suggestive; but then it is abstract, rather than personal; more of a philosophical speculation, less of a practical belief. And it leads very directly to the next side of Buddhism—what is called its Pantheistic side.

IV. Beginning with the notion that the Intelligence is entirely separated from the world; that He is One, and it multiform; the Buddhist may arrive, by a series of easy steps, at a conclusion which would seem most opposed to this, that the Intelligence is essentially one with the world: in fact, that it can only be considered as the informing life or soul of the world. As in the case of Brahminism, it may be rightly said that this

doctrine was latent in the Buddhist from the first:
in other words, that the moment he began to think
upon Nature with no other data than the belief
which he possessed, he must inevitably terminate in
this scheme. But it should be said, at the same
time, that he has struggled earnestly, even heroic-
ally, with this tendency; that his effort to contemplate the pure Essence indicates a genuine desire to
see something above the world, not merely dwelling in it, and actuating it. However true then
it may be that Buddhism often becomes a mere
notion of a God diffused through all things, I
cannot believe that this is its characteristic principle. To ascertain what that is, we must examine
the next allegation respecting it, that it is especially the deification of human saints or heroes.

V. We can scarcely speak of this as a *phase* of
Buddhism. Everywhere you will find certain human beings called Buddhas. You will find Europeans asking such questions as these, When was
Buddha born? How many Buddhas are there?
And those who are asked seem not astonished
at the inconsistency of the two enquiries, or of
either with that idea of a pure essential Intelligence, sometimes the fixed only reality, sometimes
so divested of all qualities as to become nothing,
sometimes diffused through all things. If you consider the starting point of the doctrine, you will
see that the departure from it, which is involved
in this notion of human Buddhas, is far less than
it seems. The abstracted man was to become one

with the Divinity. In the mind of the Hindoo
a whole caste is marked out for that glory. But
a whole caste evidently does not attain it; there
must be immeasurable differences of taste, earnestness. wisdom, in the priests of one generation, still
more in those of successive generations. So it
comes to pass, that there is more feeling of a Divine character diffused through a great many; less
belief of actual divinity in particular individuals.
Here, on the contrary, there is no check to the
conviction that a man has risen to the state of
Godhead—may be a God. In proportion as the
Infinite Object fades into obscurity, or waxes fearful, the vision is more cherished of his appearance
in one man, or a series of men, who in this or that
period confer blessings on some particular country,
traverse different countries; now mount into the region where Indra the Lord of the Elements dwells—
now descend to earth, like Vishnu; (for these powers
have passed from the Hindoo into the Buddhist
legends;) and leave here and there, in some mountain or valley, footmarks which may be noted, and
become the symbols of his continual presence. For
as he has moved through space, passing rapidly
from one portion of the globe to another, so does
he live through different periods of time, the same
principle inhabiting various forms; the same Buddha, though there may have been a number of
Buddhas—though they may appear even now.

VI. And now we can understand how idolatry,

the worship of different outward natural things may
be attributed to this Theistic, Atheistic, Pantheistic, human doctrine.   Through all nature, above
and beneath, Buddha has journeyed; everywhere
he has left his footmarks; everywhere we may find
tokens of him.   Sun, moon, and stars, all things
on this earth, may speak of him.   Or we may think
of him as the fixed Immoveable Past, as the Actual
Present, as the dim Future of fears and hopes.
But these sensible objects are too distant and
vague; these Past, and Present, and Future, too
abstract.   And we want to feel that we are not
contemplating them in themselves, or for their own
sakes, but the living, quickening Intelligence, which
has stamped its form upon them.   They must be
changed into symbols; in that character we must
approach them and revere them.   They must assume
shapes which are given to them by the kindred Intelligence in ourselves.

Oftentimes these shapes will be animal; for how
ought we to think of the creatures around us, with
those half human faculties and affections which we
discover in them; with the ferocity and cunning
which are surely not peculiar to them?   Must not
they be inhabited by a human spirit in some degraded, fallen condition?   Are they not wandering
about as signs to us of what we may become; of
that state to which, by cultivating the lower and
baser qualities of our nature, we may reduce ourselves?   So reasons the Buddhist; he reveres and

fears the animals as meaner forms of that Intellect, of which he sees the highest form in the glorified man, the Buddha.

VII. I have not yet spoken of Buddhism as a social system. I described its ministers as forming an *order* of devotees, as distinguished from a *caste* of priests. It is necessary to speak thus of them, for we must not suppose because they have no hereditary vocation, that they take their office at hazard, or that they have no communion with each other. We have a very accurate description of the ceremonies which are observed in some countries, at their consecration, of the questions which are asked to ascertain that they have no bodily or mental disqualification for the task. Such ceremonies, though they may vary in their forms, exist wherever Buddhism exists. In Thibet, which must be regarded as the centre and proper home of the religion, the priests are called Lamas; it is they who decide who *the* Lama, the true high priest of the universe, at any given time is. I say they decide who he is; for they could never allow that the faculty of *choosing* the chief Lama resides in them. In some person or other the spirit of Buddha dwells; he is meant to be the head of the universe; to him all owe homage. This Lama, therefore, never dies; he is lost sight of in one form, re-appears in another. The body of some old man who has had this honour loses its breath, is laid in the tomb. The Lama has passed into some infant, who is brought up in a convent with special care,

6—2

preserved from sensual influences, taught from the
cradle to look upon himself as the shrine of the Divinity, and to receive the homage of rajahs, nations,
even of the Celestial Empire; nay, even of European monarchs. Some of you may remember to
have read of a solemn embassy sent by the English government at Calcutta in the days of War-
ren Hastings to the court of the Lama. A very
affecting letter had been addressed by him to
the English authorities in India, asking their help
in checking quarrels between certain native sove-
reigns, an object, he said, which he sought diligently in prayers by day and night. An old man
was the author of this letter; before Mr. Turner,
the English envoy arrived, he had left the world;
and a child of eighteen months was acknowledged
as his successor. It reigned by no hereditary right;
but the other Lamas presented him with unques-
tioning faith as the representative of the Perfect
Intelligence through whom it would most surely
utter itself.

If we now try to sum up the evidence which
we have gathered from different indications respecting Buddhism, I do not know that we can
do it better than in the words of Mr. Hodgson,
the resident at Nepaul, to whom I have already
referred. " The one infallible diagnostic of Buddhism," he says, with an emphasis and decision
which were the result of patient enquiries, conducted during many years, " is a belief in the
infinite capacity of the human intellect." This is

the conclusion to which all our enquiries into the system have conducted us. The idea of an Adi Buddha, or Absolute Eternal Intelligence is there, but it is hidden; it gradually evaporates. The possibility of utter Atheism is there; but the heart flies in dismay from it. The vision of a Unity resulting from the reconciliation of opposites is there; but it either passes into a mere theory, or seeks for images to express it, which make it material. The conception of an intelligent soul in nature is there; but it quickly resolves itself into a recognition of all Nature, as symbolising human deeds and attributes. Lastly, the idea of deified men *is there;* but this loses itself in another, that there is in man, in humanity, a certain Divine Intelligence, which at different times and in different places, manifests itself more or less completely, and which must have some one central manifestation. The Human Intellect is first felt to be the perfect organ of worship; finally its one object. This is Buddhism; this is the conviction which, with more or less of confusion, is working in the hearts of 300 millions of people on this globe of ours.

I greatly desire to ask this doctrine, what testimony it bears for or against that hypothesis which it is the purpose of these Lectures to examine; the hypothesis, I mean, that the Divine portion of the faith of different nations signifies nothing; that it is only an attempt to explain the phenomena of the universe; that there is no need of a Revelation to man, because in him-

self, in his own heart there is a sufficient revelation of all the truths he wants to know ; that we
may safely leave this to work itself out as it can
in the different religious systems, without pretend-
ing to inculcate notions of our own, which, perhaps,
are only a little better than those we should dis-
place. But I believe we shall be in a fairer
condition to meet these questions, when we have
considered the circumstances of a country in which
Buddhism does not exist alone; in which it is
counteracted, and yet, I think, also illustrated, by
the presence of systems older, in that country at
least, than itself.

Numerous as are the puzzles which the history
and actual condition of China may present to
European enquirers—even to those few who are
acquainted with its language, and have had opportunities of closely observing it, I do not think
that there is much difference of opinion respecting
its main and distinguishing characteristic. Its
learned men, we are told by the most respectable
authorities, say, without exception, ‘a principle of
order is that which we discover and reverence in
the world :’ and every act of their lives, the con-
struction of society, their art, their most minute
ceremonies, bear out the assertion. If you hear
their choicest phrases reported to you, or look at the
works they have produced, or remember the dura-
tion of their empire, or think how many shocks
from without it has withstood, or even read one
of their singular state papers, you can scarcely

avoid saying within yourself; here is a people
which, successfully or unsuccessfully, is striving to
be orderly, which for generations has been carrying on this struggle, which hates everything that
interferes with its success, would gladly obtain
it by any sacrifice. Hence the preservation of historical records, in their driest form has been as
important a purpose in their eyes as it has been
an indifferent or impossible one to the Hindoo.
Hence, from first to last, we discover among them
precisely the opposite view of social life to that which
we have noticed in the conception of the Buddhist
Lama. The Chinese does not first ask where Spiritual Intelligence dwells, and then confess that
to this he must submit. But he starts with the
belief in government and society ; and then demands that all study and intelligence should be
applied to the preservation of it. The emperor
is the datum or postulate from which the speculations of philosophers, as well as the arrangements
of society, begin. He is put into the position
which he hold that he may be the spring and soul
of order to the commonwealth. How he may be so
he is to enquire very diligently. All the functionaries of government are to be chosen according to their fitness to preserve that order, according
to their knowledge of the maxims upon which
it rests. To prevent any infractions of it by themselves, or those over whom they rule, is to be
their incessant study. Instruction therefore, it
would seem, has been from the earliest period a

primary condition of all civil duties and employments. The Chinese have not anticipated the West
more in other machinery than in that of education,
and in the importance which they have attached to
it. Schools, great and little, especially for the
instruction of those who shall have any offices in
the state, were the great distinction of those dynas-
tics, which we should call in the history of any
other people—here the name would be strikingly
inapplicable—the heroic period of the Empire. Because they fell into decay, and the fabric of social
order with them, it was necessary that a Reformer
should appear.

Confucius appeared, not to introduce new maxims, but to revive the old—to explain what he
saw to be the conditions and first principles of
Chinese government, to embody them in books,
which have been for 2000 years the school-books
of China, the maxims of society and practical
conduct, possessing an authority higher than any
decrees, because explaining that which is to make
decrees stable, and to procure obedience to them.
The education of Confucius was one in state affairs.
He was strictly a government functionary. He
was disgusted with the confusion and disorder which
he found in all departments of the state, and he
retired to meditate in secret the grounds upon
which a reformation must be undertaken. He did
not trust solely to his own reflection, or to Chinese antiquity. There was an old man, Laoutsee,
who spoke much of the Divine Reason which dwelt

within each man, of its being the first object of
every man to cultivate this, and to bring all his
faculties of body and mind under its rule. This
he seems to have set up as the maxim of life,
in opposition to the political notions of it, which
prevailed among his countrymen generally. To
his words Confucius listened respectfully; though
far from admitting his doctrine, he turned it to
account by subordinating it to his own. He taught
also that a man must cultivate this reason in himself—must try to arrive at self-government, even
at perfect self-government; but all for social ends
and purposes, all that he might be better able to
contribute towards the rational administration of
the state; towards the preservation of public order.
But where lay the root of this order? Its first
ground Confucius, still professing only to be an
interpreter of old and admitted doctrines, said,
must lie in actual relationships; the family must
sustain the state. The authority of the father
must be the root of all other authority. The emperor must be regarded, must regard himself, as
the common father. He was set to keep his people
in order, and upon this principle he must order
himself. These were not mere words. They do
actually express that which has been the strength,
the binding principle of Chinese society, from generation to generation. Jesuit missionaries, Protestant missionaries, English travellers, French philosophical admirers of Confucius, have all alike
confessed it. The *maxims* of Confucius are faithful

results of the observations of a man honestly desirous to make use of the experience that is given him for a moral purpose; they may generally be read with interest, often with admiration, as hints for conduct—even as helps to internal self-discipline. But they would be feeble and unmeaning, and could scarcely have exercised any great influence on the mind of a nation, if they had not rested upon the recognition of a real and eternal principle of order, lying far deeper than all Chinese formalities, or than the formalities in the mind of Confucius himself. Fartherly authority was his ultimate principle. Practically, he went not a step beyond it. What he heard of divine, unseen, mysterious powers above man, or above nature, or even in man and in nature; of some thing or person above the earthly emperor, or the earthly father, he by no means denied. Whatever faith his countrymen had respecting the invisible world, he would have wished to confirm. But he did not see his way in such enquiries: he could not trace the actual connexion between them and practical life. And the sincerity of his mind revolted against the notion of merely using them as artifices to keep up respect for human institutions. On this ground he has, I think, been too hastily condemned as an atheistical philosopher. I cannot feel any desire to make good such a charge. It is a pleasanter, and also a truer course, to admit that his confession of ignorance may have been a genuine one; and may even have implied that he had deeper thoughts than he knew how to express. We may be sure that what there was weak and maimed in his scheme will discover itself in the course of history, and that this discovery will be far more valuable than any rash conclusions of ours respecting it.

Not many centuries after this reform, a Chinese emperor became aware that there was some blank in the doctrine of Confucius; a blank which was not filled up by turning him into a god, and raising temples to him. Side by side with the Confucian, or State-worship, dwelt the Taou sect, the disciples of that old philosopher with whom Confucius had conversed, men who still maintained that the Reason was something divine and mysterious in each person, and would lead him into inward contemplation, not make him the handy instrument in a State machinery. But these people had little faith, except in themselves. The effect of their mysterious knowledge upon others seemed chiefly exhibited in charms, and incantations and magic arts, which interfered with the good order of the State, rather than promoted it. Something else was wanted. The emperor heard of a great teacher and prophet somewhere in India. In spite of the remonstrances of wise men, who shewed him how grievously he was departing from Chinese maxims, in preferring foreign to native culture, the Buddhist faith was imported into the empire. A religion resting upon communion with the unseen world, in all its outward, and many of its inward characteristics, the direct opposite of the Confucian system gained footing on the soil which that system ruled. The result was what might have been expected. The new faith took hold of popular sympathy, and has retained that sympathy to the present day. It was, and is despised, by the great mandarins, by the functionaries of government, by the adorers of social order. But it is more than tolerated by the government as such; it is recognized as deserving of respect, even of homage. Though the emperor cannot allow the Lama to interfere with his own supreme rule, and has procured the appointment of a deputy Lama who shall be really the head of the Buddhist society in his dominions, and his subject, he yet sends embassies to the high priest in Thibet, and asks his intercessions for China. Evidently Buddhism is felt, even by the disciples of Confucius, to be an element of society in China, which cannot be dispensed with, and for which their own system, much as they may prefer it, offers no substitute.

I have said, that in *most* of its inward, as well as outward characteristics, the Buddhist and the Confucian doctrine are opposed. I used this language, because it is evident that in one respect they are not opposed. Different as are the functions which are assigned to the intellect of man in the three Chinese systems, that intellect is still an object of profound veneration to all. Wisdom is viewed as wholly social and experimental in one, internal and mystical in the second, strangely mixed

with the idea of what is super-human and eternal
in the third. Had it been otherwise, had there
been nothing common in these faiths, it is scarcely
possible to conceive of them dwelling together in
such an empire; or to suppose that one should at
all supply the gaps in the other.

  And which, then, of these three faiths, shall we
say can be described by that comprehensive formula, 'a mere attempt to explain the phenomena
of the universe?' All three do attempt that, doubtless,—Buddhism, especially. But, does the faith of
the Buddhist consist in this? Is it this which in
his inmost heart he wants to know? Every enquiry
we have made has led us to the opposite conclusion.
He is obliged to question the universe, because he
does not know what else he should question. He
has questioned it, and to every problem which dis-
turbs him it has returned a more confused answer.
He has asked, what that is within him which is
higher than it, what that is which seeks a knowledge which it cannot give? He is sure that he is
above the world—that it was never meant to be his
master—that the spirit in him must have its ground
elsewhere. But where? What is this ground? Is
it anything? Is it nothing? Who will tell him?
That which has asked the question cannot give the
answer. With deepest solicitude, he cries, "Do
Thou, of whom I see the footmarks in natural
things, but most of all in human beings, in those
who have thoughts, and reasons, and wills—in
those who feel that these are not meant to be

the servants of their senses, or of the things
with which their senses deal,—do Thou tell me
who Thou art, and how I may draw nigh to Thee.
Tell me what Thou hast to do with man, for something Thou must have. Tell me if there be a man,
and where he is, in whom I may behold Thee ; One
who is not here to-day, and gone to-morrow ; but
who, amidst all changes of times, the disappearance
of generations, lives on. Tell me if there be indeed a King and High Priest of the universe—a
man actually Divine. And this, too, I need to
know : What that Light is which dwells in me ;
whether it is self-derived, or, as my inward heart
tells me, derived from Thee. Whether there be
any Spirit coming forth from Thee to dwell in
men, and bind them together—to make them gentle,
and gracious, and wise—to be the common life of
all, and still the life of each. And if these things
be so, tell me how these things can be reconciled,
as my reason has whispered that it can be, though
as yet I see not how, with that Unity—the essential condition of Thy Being—that which divides
Thee from all the multitude of things and persons
with whom in this world we converse." I say that
Buddhism, rightly interpreted, is a prayer of this
kind—an earnest prayer, consciously or unconsci-
ously uttered by 300 millions of people. And yet
we are told that it is honouring the faith of these
people, shewing tenderness and respect for them,
to believe that there is not any Revelation, save
that which man procures for himself. In other

words, that this prayer never has, never can be, answered. Only if we have really brought ourselves to this contempt for the faith of so many human beings, can we patiently think of this faith working out, as the phrase is, its own results. It has been working out its results for all these thousands of years—and what have they been? The worship of the intellect has not caused the intellect to grow—not even to grow to an ordinary human or earthly stature; I say nothing of that Divine stature which it feels that it may reach. The priest of Buddha, of the Intelligence, is rarely an intelligent man. That mighty portion of the globe over which Buddhism rules is nearly the most ignorant portion of it. And yet in it lie the seeds of all highest, noblest culture, if only we can really address ourselves to that which is within the hearts of those who hold this faith, if we can only tell them that which they crave to know. That it is a vain and cruel thing merely to carry our own notions among them—our notions upon any subject, divine, human, earthly, I admit readily. If we do not know that which will solve their riddle—if we cannot tell them—Here is that which will turn doubt and confusion into clearness; here is that which is not our notion, but which has come from GOD to confound our notions, to confound our pride; and which is meant, not for us, but for mankind: for mercy's sake, let us be silent— the Buddhists are better as they are.

So also of the Confucian scheme. That cannot
be charged with want of practical results. Yet that
something is wanting, China itself has confessed.
Can it be supplied from within? When we fancy
it I think we commit a great injustice. Mr. Medhurst, the author of an interesting book on China,
the result of his own observations, expresses his
wonder, and even indignation, that Confucius, having dwelt so beautifully on the rights and duties of
a father, should not have carried up his thoughts to
the Great Father of all. I confess that I feel quite
unable to adopt this language. It seems to me evidence of Confucius being a sincere man, that he did
not allow himself to use mere figures of rhetoric
upon this subject, for such in his lips they would
have been. If having spoken of one holding an
actual relation under the name of Father, he had
afterwards used that word as a synonym for a Creator or for an unknown Being, the pleasure which
such expressions might have caused us would have
been dearly purchased by the loss of reality in the
mind of him who resorted to them. If you can tell
the Chinese that this is an actual relation, that
it has been proved to be so, that our human
relation is the image of it, that the reality of
one gives reality to the other, that the honour
paid to relationships is not incompatible with that
seemingly abstract, unsocial, unreal view of the
Reason of which the Taou sect has been the champion; and that the Buddhist spiritualism is not

an .element of new confusion, but of reconciliation—
you will indeed discover to him that deepest foundation of order which he is looking for—you will shew
him that way from the visible to the Invisible which
he has never yet discovered. But any teaching
short of this, that hard and formal and yet withal
practical and serious, mind of his, will repel. You
will find that you have not learnt the spell which
can break the heavy yoke of custom from off his
neck, and change him from the most perfect of
living machines into a living MAN.

———

LECTURE IV.

The Mahometan, the Hindoo, and the Buddhist, are the great prevailing faiths of the world. A person indeed who should insist upon reducing all the religious thoughts and convictions he met with in different places under one of these three heads, would exhibit great practical ignorance; for the feelings and apprehensions which belong to actual human beings will not bear to be so treated. A man will not really be intelligible to you, if, instead of listening to him and sympathising with him, you determine to classify him. But it is true, that one who has patiently studied and livingly realized the characteristics of these wide-spread beliefs, will not be hopelessly puzzled by the notions of men in any part of the globe, civilized or savage. There are no other existing forms of religious thought sufficiently distinct from these to deserve a separate examination in such a course as this; none which have not grown out of them, or have not been rapidly absorbed into them. And it is of existing systems that I wished first and chiefly to speak, because for the practical object I proposed to myself, and which Boyle desired we should keep in sight, these must be the most important. I could not, however, do proper justice to the subject if, before

I enter upon the second division of it—the consideration of the way in which Christianity is
related to different religions—I did not touch
upon what may be called the defunct systems,
those which belong to history, and which have
yielded to the might either of the Crescent or the
Cross. The word ' defunct,' we shall soon find, is
only in one sense applicable to them; they had that
in them which is not dead, and cannot die; that
which is exerting an influence upon the mind and
education of Christendom at the present day. Still,
as systems, they belong to the past; they will
therefore supply a new kind of test for trying
the maxims respecting the worthlessness and tran-
sitoriness of what is merely theological, which I
have been examining in former Lectures. For
the reason I have given they ought not to be
treated in the same detail as those which have
occupied us hitherto: indeed, I do not think we
should gain so much by considering them in detail,
as by glancing at them side by side; so that the
principles which distinguish them, and those wherein
they are alike, may be more readily discerned. I
shall therefore endeavour to compress what I have
to say of them into a single Lecture.

I. The old Persian religion is the first which
offers itself to our notice, as standing in a close
relation, both outwardly and inwardly, to the Hindoo. The Zendavesta, the religious book in which
this faith is professedly set forth, cannot be appealed to as a very certain authority respecting

7—2

it ; what we possess is confessedly a compilation from earlier sources; and though critics think that they can detect older fragments in the midst of it, there is great difficulty in separating them from the mass, or in determining the time when it was put together. The age and history of the man who is spoken of as the great prophet of this faith, Zerdusht or Zoroaster, are equally obscure. It has even been questioned whether such a man ever existed—whether he does not merely represent a divine principle, or a stage in a nation's history. It might seem, then, as if this doctrine, of which we have such vague records, must have exercised but a slight influence ; at all events, that its essential character cannot be ascertained. Both conclusions would be erroneous. Whatever authority the Zendavesta may have, whatever kind of person Zoroaster may have been, the Persian faith has been bound up with the life of a great portion of Asia, and has left as strong evidences as any both of its nature and of its power over the minds of men, even in generations far removed from each other.

The readers of Gibbon will remember a splendid passage of his history describing a great Asiatic revolution which took place in the third century after Christ. The old Persian empire was then ruled by the Parthians. Their dynasty had lasted for several centuries: it had been set up after the Greek armies had conquered Asia ; after they had established their own habits and civi-

lization in the midst of it.   Their worship the Parthians to a considerable extent adopted; the old
faith of the Persians they crushed.   At the period
I speak of it was found that this faith had lain
hidden under the soil, but had never been destroyed.
The Magi came forth and proclaimed that which
they affirmed to be the original teaching of Zoroaster.   The innovations of five centuries were swept
away—a dynasty which the Persians recognized
as the continuation of the old kingdom of Cyrus
was established, and the nation's old belief was
the foundation upon which it rested.   This power
became the great Eastern antagonist of Rome:
at a later period, it had nearly wrested the empire of Asia from Constantinople: it sunk at last
under the irresistible strength of the Mahometan
armies.   For a time, those whom the Mahometans
called fire-worshippers struggled hard: at length
they vanished into an insignificant sect; Persia
acknowledged the Prophet of Arabia as its one
divine teacher.

But what was the faith which governed the old
Persian while he ruled the world—which dwelt so
deeply in the heart of a people that it could revive
after a lapse of centuries—which perished all but
utterly at last?   We have seen that the Brahm of
the Hindoo, the Buddha of that mighty sect which
arose out of Hindooism, is especially the Intelligent
Being, He in whom light dwells, and by communication with whom men become enlighened.   Observe
how naturally, how inevitably, one uses this word

Light for Intelligence. We feel instinctively that
it is much the better word of the two; that one is
hard and abstract, the other living and real. So
men have felt in all countries and ages. Their bodily
eye distinguished one thing from another—could
exert itself in the day, was useless in darkness.
They had as certainly something within them which
could discern a sense in words, a meaning in
things. This surely was an eye too. There was
no better way of speaking about it. And there
must be some light answering to this eye, older
than it, otherwise it could not be. They discovered,
too surely also, that there was a state in which
this eye saw nothing, a state of darkness. If we
keep these very simple thoughts in our minds,
(I say, keep them in our minds, for they are there
already; we are obliged to make use of this language—it belongs to us all, to prince and peasant
alike); and if we recollect that what we are apt
to overlook as too simple, is oftentimes just the
most important thing of all—the key which un-
locks a multitude of treasure-houses, we shall be
able to enter into the belief of different people,
and to trace the transition from one to another
far more easily. The conviction which we have
found dwelling so strongly in the minds of Brahmin and Buddhist, though taking different forms,
was this—'he who has the inward eye most opened,
must be the greatest man: he in whom it is
quenched, must be the lowest and most miserable
man.' And the puzzle which we saw tormenting

them both, in different ways and different degrees,
was this. But where *is* this light? Is it only in
the eye? What then does the eye behold? Is
it *not* in the eye? How then can I call that a
light? A very deep question indeed; the answers
to which, in every case, are full of practical sig-
nificance. The Persian solution was the most simple
of all. He felt that his whole life was precisely
this debate between light and darkness. There
must, he said, be Lords over this light and darkness. This had probably been his oldest and strongest conviction.

The nights in Persia are clear and beautiful.
The stars were a language which spoke to peasant and priest alike of light coming out of darkness. On these the one will have meditated till
he thought them powers and rulers of the world;
the other will have paid them actual homage. The
Magians, the servants of the Light, will have
devised a system of worship addressed to these.
If Zerdusht or Zoroaster were a real man, he probably arose at a time when this worship had become
very general, and when the mind of the people had
become much debased by it. To some man, or
some men, it was given to perceive that the ministers of light had become ministers of darkness.
Those things which testified of a Divine Light had
been substituted for it. He rose up as the witness
for Ormuzd, the Lord of Light, to testify that
light comes from him, and not from the outward,

material things; that whoso serves them is the
servant of Ahriman, the Prince of Darkness. While
Ahriman teaches his servants to bow down before
visible things, Ormuzd communicates to men his
living Word, (that is the meaning of Zendavesta,)
speaks to their hearts, teaches them the laws of
justice and order. The battle between Ormuzd
and Ahriman will be long, but Ormuzd must triumph
at last. The kingdom of light is mightier than
the kingdom of darkness. This was the substance
of the Persian faith, to the revival of which, in
its strength and simplicity, all that was vigorous
in the Persian character and government, seems to
have been owing. There was the greatest difference between it and the Hindoo—precisely this
difference. The Hindoo thought of light and darkness as the opposition between cultivation and ignorance—between the Brahmin and the Sudra; the
Persian looked upon them as expressions for *right*
and *wrong*. Far less refined and intellectual than
the Indian, far less capable of mere speculation, he
had a sense of practical, moral distinctions, to
which the other was almost a stranger, or, at
least, which never presented themselves to him,
nakedly and directly, as the foundation of all other
distinctions. Hence a difference in their scheme of
life. Right must be proclaimed by some one ; not
merely recognized or perceived. The Persian, therefore, looked much more to an authority which
should command men, or to a teacher who should

impart wisdom, than merely to a thinker or devotee.
He regarded the king, from whom the law and
words of grace proceeded, with more reverence
than the priest. There might be many conflicts
between the two, at times they might work in harmony, but this was the abiding, characteristic
Persian feeling.

But there were two or three difficulties specially
besetting him who held this faith. The Persian
felt that visible things were not to be adored. It
was the worship of Ahriman to set up them as the
lords of men. Yet he had more need than the
Hindoo to feel that the object he was worshipping
was above himself, not merely *in* himself. He must
speak of the Light as coming to him, not merely
as proceeding from him. But if so, how shall he
realize it? Must not the light, or must not the
fire, or must not the sun, be in some sense or other
an object for him to fear and obey? This thought
would be always re-appearing in the popular mind,
nay, in the mind of the teacher who most protested
against it, when he was struggling with the tendency in himself and other men to set up their own
thoughts as if the true Light was in them. To meet
it the Magian devises a theory. These outward
objects are but images or counterfeits of something
within; they are the productions of the king of darkness: the good and great beings who appear in the
world come forth from the inner kingdom to subvert
these. Starting from such a notion as this, it was
easy to produce a universe of phantasies, against

which the simple and earnest mind of the Persian,
struggling, and struggling in vain, would plunge into
direct idolatry.   Another awful question there was:
Did this power of good originate the power of evil,
or is each self-created?   Or whence do they come?
Some hidden being there must be—some deeper
ground than all that man could conceive.   They
tried to express it in some name—they called this
ground of all things, *Time without Bounds.*

Under this last form the Persian faith came into
contact with the Christian Church of the first ages.
The influence of the Gospel over Persia was slight
and partial; but the preachers of it perceived a
deep meaning in the Persian speculations.   Gradually some appeared who thought the speculation
beautiful, who cared little for the solution.   These
produced some of the darkest of the early heresies.
When the Mussulman encountered the Persian
faith he felt no such temptation.   "Is this your
GOD—this Time without bounds, this phantasy
the Living Being?   It is impossible.   No! pretend what you will, you are worshippers of fire,
or of the sun, or of the stars.   With our swords
we cut through your webs of sophistry—through
your worlds seen and unseen—your good and your
evil principles.   There is one GOD, and Mahomet
is his prophet.   Yield to that belief, or perish!"

The victory was very complete; such an one is
hardly recorded in the annals of the world.   But
when it was effected there was found to be something imperishable in Persian faith and feelings

which could change the characteristics of Mahometanism itself. To it we owe those stories of fairies
and genii, which mix with our earliest impressions
of Mahometanism, though they certainly have no
natural connexion with it. In a later time Persia
became the home of the great Sofi schism, which
has introduced a new Pantheistic element into
the doctrine of the Koran. Under the Mahometan teaching, which in Turkey has certainly been
favourable to veracity, the strong sense of moral
right and wrong which distinguished the Old
Persian has deserted him. He who was celebrated
by Xenophon as above all men the speaker of truth,
has become proverbial for lying.

II. The history of Persia at a certain period becomes connected with that of Egypt. The connexion is a religious one. The Persian king, Cam-
byses, seems to have been a fanatic, and to have
carried on wars, if not for the propagation of his own
faith, at least, for the punishment of those who held
what he thought a false one. The Egyptian priests
were especial objects of his abhorrence. If we ask on
what grounds, we shall be led into the consideration
of another faith of the old world, which has left the
most singular records of itself; which at different
periods of its existence is bound up with Jewish and
with Greek history ; which was an object of profound interest to students 2000 years ago, and is
scarcely of less interest to the students of our own
century.

One subject immediately suggests itself to most

of us when we think of Egypt. I mean its hiero-
glyphics, or sacred symbolical writing. And as the
deciphering of this writing has been the key to
all modern discoveries respecting the details of the
history of this people, so the mere fact itself that
they did use such a character, is, perhaps, the most
helpful of all to the understanding of its principle.
We have seen what a puzzle it was to the Persian to connect the outward things which he saw
with those which were objects of his thought; how
continually there seemed to be some light very
near to his mind and heart which was revealing
itself to him; how while he realized this conviction, the outward sensible things which with-
drew him from this light, were regarded as dark
and evil; and yet how difficult he found it to
express his thoughts about that inward light,
except in terms which soon became confused with
sensible images. The Egyptian never seems to
have had this horror of visible things. He felt
that something very sacred lay beneath them, and
was expressed by them. To discover what this
was, to read what was hidden in the objects of
nature, was, in his apprehension, the function of the
wise man. Then he was to translate back these
perceptions of his, into outward forms and images,
that the vulgar might be able to profit by them
so far as it was meant that they should. Hence,
there grew up an order of priests in Egypt, as separate from the rest of society, as the Brahmins. A
caste system organized itself in the African, as in

the Asiatic nation. But the Egyptian priest was
not an abstracted man in the same sense as the
Hindoo; he did not so much withdraw himself
from the contemplation of outward things, as seek
to extract a virtue and a meaning from them. His
first thought of all seems to have been that there
was a Being hidden from man, but who was making himself manifest in different forms and signs.
His operations in nature, the power which is exerted over the earth, and the life which goes on
within it, might, especially in a country of such
unparalleled fertility as Egypt, present themselves
as objects of wonder and witnesses of a Divine
presence. But it would be impossible to think
of these powers in the earth, without thinking of
the animals which dwell upon it—of the different
powers and qualities which they display, of their
birth, and decay and renewal. These animals supply him more distinct and definite symbols than
the vague expanse of the heaven or earth. Different kinds of power are more concentrated and
expressed in them; they can be far more easily
exhibited in stone or in writing. Hence these
became predominant objects of meditation to the
priests. The various characteristics of the Godhead very soon become Gods. Students of Egyptian monuments discover three stages in the worship
—three different cycles of gods. In the earliest
cycle the idea of the Ammon, the hidden god, is
the predominant one; and his manifestations are
themselves rather in active energies, in vital opera-

tions, than in outward objects. The third cycle is
the one most directly outward, hinting, however, at
principles which in the first period were less perceived. As might be expected, different cities are
found to have different classes of symbols; those in
Upper Egypt to be characteristically diverse from
those in the Lower; though at some period an
attempt must have been made to bring all into one
system.

Here, then, we seem to be in *the* idolatrous
country—the country of divided worship: that which
teaches us what idolatry means; how man loses sight
of a centre: how every separate thing about him may
become his master. And yet, throughout the whole
of this idolatry there is a perpetual questioning of
an unknown power to tell what this visible creation
means. Each thing that is beheld is a riddle, an
oppressive, tormenting riddle, of which some solution
must be found. The Egyptian priest feels that
the riddle is *in* the things. He does not put it
into them, and it is not for him to do more than
catch a stray hint of what each is denoting But
there is some object, some centre. The Pyramids
point up to heaven as if they would say, " We are
in search of it, we would reach it if we could."

Such a system as this, on whatever side he
viewed it, would be very offensive to a Persian
king, especially if he lived shortly after the revival
of his own faith, and before it had undergone any
of its later changes. The Egyptians would seem
to him worshippers of those outward things, which

he was taught to regard as in some sort the possessions of Ahriman. And all their mystical wisdom
would look like miserable attempts to bring light
out of darkness.   It was far otherwise with the
Greek.   The enquiries and speculations of the
Egyptian priests were listened to by him with
attention and wonder.   He thought they had a
secret which he did not possess; he eagerly, but
often in vain, questioned them to learn what it
was.   In later times, when a Greek kingdom had
established itself in the heart of Egypt, under the
Ptolemies, both Jews and Greeks met upon that
soil, and the old Egyptian feeling, of a mysterious
meaning lying at the root of all things, exercised
a remarkable influence over both.   The influence
was felt by the Christian Church which established
itself afterwards there, and which consisted of both
elements.   It has left deep traces in the thoughts
of men during all subsequent periods.   But Christianity, which had a strong hold upon the Greek
cities of Egypt, seems never to have penetrated
into the heart of the country population.   The
symbolizing tendencies which it had inherited from
the old faith led to divisions on most momentous
points, which appeared to lose their momentousness
in the violent party strifes and intellectual subtleties to which they gave rise.   Egypt became sec-
tarian and demoralized; the Mahometan power
established itself there.   Various dynasties and various forms of Islamism have possessed it at different
times; the arms which swept away subtleties and

janglings were utterly unable to cultivate the mind
of the Egyptian. All the European refinements
and material wisdom of its present ruler have not
awakened one thought in the people's heart, or
done ought but make their slavery more ignominious and hateful. If the Memnon lyre is again
to give forth any music, it must be touched by
the rays from some sun which is not yet visible
in that heaven.

III. To understand the difference between the
Egyptian and the Greek faith, it is not necessary
to study a great many volumes, or to visit different
lands: our own British Museum will bring the
contrast before us in all its strength. If we pass
from the hall of Egyptian antiquities into the room
which contains the Elgin marbles, we feel at once
that we are in another world. The oppression of
huge animal forms, the perplexity of grotesque
devices, has passed away. You are in the midst
of human forms, each individually natural and
graceful, linked together in harmonious groups;
expressing perfect animal beauty, yet still more
the dominion of human intelligence over the animal.
You perceive that the Greek is not mainly occupied with spelling out a meaning in the forms
of nature: their symmetry and harmony present
themselves to him as delightful and satisfying.
He is not trying to find out the natural characters in which he shall utter his thoughts: he
feels that he is able to write them in a character devised by themselves, upon nature. He

can take the forms of the world and mould them into expressions of the spirit that is working in himself. The Brahm or Buddha of the East, the God of Intelligence, is with him. At Delphi, the centre of the world, He utters his oracles of wisdom, by which states and men are to rule themselves. But he is no mere formal, abstract Divinity: He is all Light like the Persian divinity; you may see him in the sun; but he himself is a beautiful human being, with his quiver and bow, destroying the creatures that offend the earth, or punishing human wrongs; with the lyre, at the sound of which cities spring up and men are brought into order and harmony. Apollo seems to be the central figure in Greek mythology, that around which the others have disposed themselves. The idea of Light and Wisdom, which is concentrated in him, is diffused in different forms, male and female, through the rest of the mythology, each having some particular locality, and presenting some different aspect to the Greek mind.

But it is felt that this bright, clear, human form cannot be the ground of all things. A Hindoo might have said that he was an emanation from the First Principle; but a Greek, with his strong human feelings, at once refers him to a Parent, says that he must be the Son of Zeus, the Lord of All. And what is He, and where does He dwell? On a high Thessalian hill, out of the sight of men. There his thunders are heard; thence his decrees come forth. An awe

surrounds his habitation, but He too very speedily
becomes a clear, definite conception. He is beheld
in a human form, presently figured in sculpture.
Human acts and passions are ascribed to him. The
thought of mere solitary, self-subsisting grandeur
is intolerable to the Greek: around him therefore must be a council of chiefs. And since the
upper world seems his possession, since it is impossible to conceive of him otherwise than in the
World of Light, the nether world, the dark world,
must have its own ruler, and that other strange
region, which seems neither to belong to the world
above nor to the world below, the illimitable ocean,
on which the Greek gazed with delight and child-
like wonder, which was ready to swallow him up,
and yet which owned his rule, which he could
traverse with his ships, which gave him a sense
of unbounded freedom and communion, even while
it shut him in, and separated him from his fellows—
this too must have its ruler.

There was delight in forming these conceptions,
in moulding them into actual shapes; and yet the
heart craved for something else, something that
it could not thus conceive and mould. Dreams
came to them of an earlier period, when another
divinity, older than Zeus, had dominion—Chronos,
or Time, was his name. Of such a one Zoroaster
had spoken, but his abstraction of time without
limits is quickly moulded by the Greek into an outward form—an old man with a scythe, who devours
his children so soon as they are born. So soon did

these visions of a world above man, or of a world
in the past, take their shape and colouring from
the actual world, and from the mind of him who
observed it.   And other visions there were, which
confessedly belonged to earth, though they began
and ended with heaven.   The Greek Hercules is
the head of a whole class of human benefactors
and heroes, who tilled and subdued the earth,
drained marshes, destroyed beasts and oppressive
men, one of whom also penetrated into the lower
world, delivered the victims of death, so proving his title to be a son of the god, and, ultimately, rising into fellowship with the gods.   With
these were mingled men who aspired rashly and
presumptuously to that glory—Titans, who strove
to overcome the Lord of Heaven by pure strength—
one who was sentenced to perpetual thirst for
seizing the divine nectar—one whose name declares him to be the representative of wisdom
and foresight, who opposed the brute strength
of the Titans, but who, because he stole fire from
heaven for the good of man, must be fastened to
a rock, and be the prey of a vulture, till a pre-
destined deliverer should come.

All these conceptions could harmonize very well
with that worship of Apollo which seems to have
been characteristically the Greek worship.   But
at some time or other a mysterious divinity appeared, who possessed men with an inspiration
which raised them into gods, or degraded them
into brutes—a power to be felt rather than be-

8—2

held. The Greek imagination was able to give
even this Deity a form and a name; to invest him
with ivy-leaves, and describe him as coming amid
songs and shoutings from India. But the idea of
such a power, so near to man, so deep and inward,
could not forsake them. It uttered itself in poems,
which were of a very different character from the
free songs of early times; which spoke of man
as carrying on a conflict with himself and with
the world ; which spoke of a deep, unknown Fate,
whereto even the gods must bow. This faith associated itself also with mysteries, which imparted
to the mind of the whole nation a sense of something most sacred, which no words could utter,
or images represent, and which must, nevertheless,
lie at the root of human life and society.

Meantime the feelings which these mysteries
conveyed to the popular mind were realized in another way by thoughtful men ; they began to say
within themselves, The origin of the things we
see, of our own lives, of human society, cannot be
in those persons to whom the traditions of our
ancestors have ascribed them. The·authors, they
said, of these traditions were poets, who created
our creators. But where is that which is not conceived, not created? Is it in the things themselves—in water, or earth, or air, or fire? Is it in
our own mind? Is it in some principle which
unites these together? These were the questions
which the Greeks asked themselves, when they
could be no longer content with the vision of a

fair-haired Apollo, but must find out what that
Light or Intelligence was of which he testified.
In pursuing such enquiries, some were willing to
ask aid of those Egyptian priests who seemed to
have discerned the meaning of things, and not to
have invented a meaning for them. Some sought
to turn the stories of their childhood into mere
abstract speculations; some discarded them, and
all belief together. The wisest of them laboured
to shew them that their consciences and reason did
demand something which they did not create for
themselves; that all faith and reverence and worship, the words which they spoke—their own existence—their very doubts and questionings, pointed
to a deep, eternal ground, which could not be a
visible phantom, nor a theory, nor an abstraction—
which must be *the* Being.

We may easily perhaps persuade ourselves that
with this record of human thoughts we have nothing to do. But with it is bound up the history of one of the most remarkable people that
has ever existed upon the earth. This inward
history is necessary to interpret the outward one.
From it we must learn why the Greeks were so
mighty, and why they were so weak, why their
intellect asserted such a dominion over the greatest
physical power, and why it could not be victorious
over the animal nature in themselves, why, when
they were feeble, they seemed capable of ruling
the world, and why, when they became its masters,
they were broken in pieces. And this enquiry has

not become an obsolete one even in reference to
Greece itself: the last thirty years have given it
new interest. The Greek mythology, after some
desperate efforts to ally itself with philosophy, and
in that shape to put itself forth as an antagonist
to Christianity, sunk into insignificance; the last
school of purely Greek philosophy was closed in the
reign of Justinian. But the habits and character
which that mythology and philosophy embodied,
exhibited themselves most remarkably in the history and controversies of the Christian church,
were preserved at Constantinople through the whole
of the middle ages, penetrated into the West at
the revival of letters, have survived on their own
soil three centuries of Mahometan dominion, and
must be earnestly studied by all who desire that
the new Greek kingdom should not exhibit all the
vices and none of the merits of the old Greek re-
publics; who desire that it should be, as it may be,
an efficient bond between the European and the
Asiatic, the Western and the Eastern World.

IV. The Faith which is embodied in the acts
and literature of the Romans is often supposed to
be the same with that of the Greeks. But this opinion arises, I think, from the habit of comparing
the systems together, instead of seeking the main
and central object in each. The majority of the
Latin books which we read belong to a period after
the Greeks had become the teachers of Rome, and
after its own faith had in a great measure disappeared. Yet even from these, it is easy to perceive

that Apollo, who, as the teacher of wisdom, the
model of human beauty, the source of harmony,
was the prominent Greek Divinity, never could
have occupied any similar place in the Latin mind.
In the *system* of the Greeks the father of gods and
men was of course the centre.   He was so, I think,
practically and vitally to the Roman.   But *he* did
not habitually think of Jupiter as seated on a
mountain, as the lord of earth and air. Such notions
might gradually develope themselves in his mind;
but, first of all, he believed there was one in the
capitol of his own city; a presence there from
which all law and government, the right of the
father, the authority of the consul, proceeded. This
idea of a Being not dwelling somewhere in the
centre of the world, and uttering oracles of wisdom,
to guide the thoughts and understandings of men,
but dwelling in the centre of the City, and issuing
words of authority and law to bind citizens together, to restrain, mould, organize societies, seems
to mark the difference between the characters and
doings of the two nations; each wonderfully asserting the power of man over natural things, and
ascribing this power to his connexion with a divine
ruler, or teacher, or inspirer: but the one using
nature to set forth man's thoughts, the other
making it the servant of his purposes; the first
creating statues, the other, roads and aqueducts;
both aiming at unity, but the one always ready
to sacrifice actual unity to an ideal, the other
considering everything subordinate to that of keep-

ing men practically at one; each alike disturbed
by the oppositions of selfwill and individual interest; but these concealing themselves, in the
Greek, under the pretence of defending some principle; in the Roman, under the appearance of
upholding the rights of some order.

This distinction is apparent in every part of
the Roman faith. A god who defines and preserves
boundaries is more sacred in his eyes than the
teacher of the divinest art. If he honours any
being as a teacher it is Mercury, because he imparts
the gift of eloquence, by which bodies of men
are swayed—by which armies are moved or regu-
lated. This result, and not the cultivation of any
faculty for its own sake, is what he seeks from
the god. The god of war, who is often utterly
contemptible in the Greek legends, is his great
patron and defender. The first king in old Roman
heroic traditions is his son, though it is not as
a conqueror, but as the organiser of an infant community, that those traditions present him to us.
War, in the Roman conception of it, is not an
exhibition of individual prowess, however such prowess may be called forth by it: but a means of
subduing restless, striving atoms into order. It is,
then, not at all inconsistent with his reverence for
Mars, that a feeling of the sanctity of domestic ties,
should especially belong to his faith. Virgil, who
though as a writer he may have copied Greek
models, was in heart a Roman, and entered into
the spirit of his country's traditions better than

most men, lays the foundation of it in filial reverence, in the care of household gods. If the Roman entertained any of the Persian awe of fire,
as the symbol of light and penetrating power, it
was expressed in his worship of Vesta, the goddess
of the hearth, the preserver of family purity, and
in the fire which was ever to be kept burning
within her temple. The power of the father lay
at the root of his law and life; and it was not,
like the Chinese, a mere human apprehension, it
was practically and essentially connected with all
his thoughts of a Divine Being. He looked upon
the bonds of family life as implied in the existence of a compact commonwealth—as its necessary
basis and continual support. Upon any less real
foundation so mighty a power could not have
stood. Having such a ground, whatever threatened
it with dissolution ultimately contributed to its
strength. Conflicts of different orders of society
brought out principles of the constitution which
were previously latent; opposing principles, yet necessary to each other. And soon it seemed as if
a power which had grown up by such regular
and mysterious processes must be irresistible. Car-
thage, Egypt, Greece, bowed before it. The Parthian empire disputed with it the sovereignty of
Asia. The countries of Western Europe it appeared
specially appointed to subdue and civilize. The Belief of Rome gave it, as we have seen, its centre;
in the capitol where Jove dwelt, the nation and
the world which it ruled found the principle of

its cohesion. The statesmen saw that it was so; they lost the belief, but determined that it must be upheld for the state's sake. Family life they would have acknowledged it was expedient to uphold for the same reason; but that refused to stand upon a fiction, to live merely because it was wanted by the politician. As all the bonds of it were relaxed, the forms of the religion became more consciously unreal. And then it was seen that the state could not exist any longer upon its old ground. A visible Emperor must supply the place of an invisible Law and Presence. The military sacrament of the soldiers to the commander must be the one substitute for the old reverence. And such was the force of this bond, so much of the old feeling and principle of order still survived in it, that the state could last even for centuries with this thin plank separating it from the abyss. The plank cracked often—gave way utterly at last; and the nations, which had been prepared for the day and the hour, seized the spoil. Before that catastrophe the proclamation of a set of Galilean fishermen, that a crucified man was the Lord of the World, had been believed by the Emperors. Roman paganism seemed to disappear from the earth. But its peculiar character, the secret of its power, the cause of its decay, should be carefully reflected on, or the history of Western Christendom for 1200 years will be to us an inexplicable riddle.

V. Very soon after Rome became an empire it

was discovered that there was a part of Europe
which was more formidable to it than even the
Parthian empire in the East. Intelligent Romans began to enquire very earnestly what that
German race was which seemed to present the
newest and strangest obstacle to Roman ascendency. They had a prophetic feeling that the
question would be a very interesting one in after
days to their own country and to mankind. They
found a people who recalled to them the traditions
of their own ancestors; rude and scattered, full
of individual energy, severe and chaste, reverencing
family bonds ; with a sense, however imperfectly
developed, of social order. A few observations they
made upon the faith of this people, which are well
worthy of note. " The Germans looked upon day,"
says Tacitus, " as coming out of night, the last as
the ground of the first. They appeared to pay a
kind of worship to the earth. They looked upon
themselves as descended from Mannus." It seemed
to the Roman, trying to translate their notions into
his own, that Mercury was their chief god. These
hints, slight and imperfect as they are, throw great
light upon the mythology of Germany and the
North, as we receive it from those who lived under
its influence. To trace it through all its mazes may
be difficult, and not very profitable ; but there are
certain great features in it which are worthy of
earnest consideration.

The feeling of light and darkness, as two opposing worlds, is as strong among the Gothic people

as it was among the Persians. Perhaps there was
this difference ; Darkness might be regarded as the
invader by one, Light by the other. You would
perhaps expect as much from the climate and
atmosphere of Iran, as compared with that of
Sweden or Norway; and hence you might easily
pass to the conclusion, that the mythology of one,
or both, has merely to do with the physical world,
merely embodies the observations of men about the
heavenly bodies and their influences upon the earth,
or the processes that go on in its womb. Doubtless, these observations may be traced everywhere.
The phænomena of the world occasioned the Northerns deepest perplexity; all the powers of earth
and air, and fire and water, are at work in their
tales and poems. The conflicts of these powers
may, in one sense, be said to be the subject of
them. The sea commonly seems to be contemplated as that out of which all things have emerged.

But we know little, indeed, about our ancestors,
if we suppose that they were thinking merely about
such matters. They described wars of giants, of
good and evil powers. It is easy to say these
giants only express the struggles and throes of
nature—life contending with death, spring suc-
ceeding winter. But why are they giants? Why
do they take this personal form ? Why, if winter
and spring were chiefly in their minds, did they not
speak of winter and spring? Tacitus is most right
in saying that the earth is the object of their
study, perhaps, of their worship; but he is still

more right in saying that they felt themselves
derived from Mannus. Man is the subduer of the
earth ; because he lives upon it, tills it, sows it,
rescues it from the waters, brings the harvests
of autumn out of the frosts of winter, therefore
do these Northerns care about the earth. And those
battles which they see going on upon it, or beneath it, those struggles of gigantic powers of
evil with deliverers and benefactors, are interpreted
to them by what they feel going on in themselves ;
they are the wars of Mannus, much more than of
the earth, and sea, and sky. Read them in this
light, and every Northern saga is full of profoundest
interest and instruction. A mighty power of death
and of darkness struggling to draw all creatures
into itself; mightier powers of good struggling
against it : consuming fires, that are to destroy
what is corrupt ; life coming out of death, second
birth, resurrection—these are ideas by which you
see that they were haunted and possessed. They
could find no clue to the strange mystery, yet they
felt that it was near them, and about them, and
that there must be some bright sun, which would
come forth one day to scatter the shadows, and
shew all things in their true relations and propor-
tions. But yet it is equally true that Mannus himself and his origin are lost in the Infinite. Tacitus
expresses the idea of the mythology in this respect
too distinctly and definitely, but not unhappily,
when he speaks of Mercury, the messenger of
gods and men, who passes rapidly from heaven
to earth, and from earth to the shades below, who

connects each with the other, as the object of
Gothic reverence. Such a being, only surrounded
with vagueness and mist, not capable of being exhibited in a form like the Greek Hermes, or the
Roman Mercury, is the Northern Odin. Each
new theorist about him will present him in a different aspect, one as a mere mortal, to whom a
history may be ascribed—one as a mere Divinity—
one as a teacher of human wisdom—one as merely
the ideal of wisdom—one perhaps as the representation of some physical process—one as the es-
tablisher of a political order. Each may give
plausible reasons for his opinion; no worshipper
of him could have told you which was true; he
would have felt that in some sense all must be
true. Precisely the necessity of his mind was to
find some object in which these characters might
really meet: who should bring the clear light out
of the darkness, and be a conqueror in that war
with the earth's tormentors.

———————

I have now completed this division of my subject, and I may ask you for a moment to consider
how the different portions of it are connected together, and what is the general result. Mahometanism, we see, stands upon a different ground from
all the rest. It starts from the Divine Will, it
assumes a declaration of that Will to men, it
affirms men to be the servants of God to execute
His Will. Hindooism has only the faintest conception of a Divine Will; but it recognizes a

Divine original Light or Intelligence from which
the intelligence in man proceeds, and which it
is to contemplate. In striving to ascertain what
this Light is—how it is distinct from the human
intelligence—the Brahmin becomes lost in speculation. The Buddhist cuts the knot, practically
makes man's intellect the origin of all things; yet
recognizes a certain universal Intelligence dwelling
in the race, and concentrated from time to time
in some person. Hindooism and Buddhism have
been compelled in different ways to come down
from the merely abstract region, and to speak of the
Divinity as concerned with the doings of ordinary
men; as exercising influences beneficent or per-
nicious over them : each has been obliged to explain what the universe has to do with the original
Intelligence ; each has been compelled into an
idolatry of material things, against which, in its
first conception, it is a protest. Both have struggled with Mahometanism, and been overcome by
it; neither has been able to amalgamate with it,
for neither has it been found to be a substitute.
Buddhism in China has established itself side by
side with a system of social order, the basis of
which is the recognition of paternal authority, and
which regards the knowledge of the invisible as
unattainable. Entirely opposed to this system,
Buddhism has been found nevertheless an indispensable supplement to it; even for the accom-
plishment of its own purpose. These different
faiths which exercise a dominion over so large a

portion of the universe, do claim something to
satisfy them, something to unite them. Not one
of them contains the solution of the difficulties
which it has raised; each testifies that there is
a chasm which the other seems meant to fill up;
but it remains a chasm still. Not one of them can
be satisfied by any philosophical theory about the
universe, or about man, or about God, or about
all of them. Mahometanism meets all such substi-
tutions by its primary proclamation, God is; He
must be a living personal Being: he must be the
King of Men. Hindooism is continually attempting
to philosophize, but every new turn of its history
proclaims, We want a Living Intelligence, which
shall hold converse *with* men, and with which men
may converse. Buddhism has been a continual
effort at philosophy; but every passage of its history proclaims, Theories will not do for us; we
want a Living Intelligence to dwell *in* man. And
now we have to add some new evidence to this.
First, we hear from Persia a cry for some infinite, absolute Being, the ground of Light and
Darkness, which he can only call Illimitable Time.
Then from the Egyptian the witness of an Ammon, or hidden God. Then from the Greek the
cry for something which he cannot express—which
must be veiled in mysteries, which the poet speaks
of as irresistible fate, which the philosopher says
must be the Being, which cannot be material, and
yet is no abstraction. The Roman must have an
invisible God of the city, a righteous lawgiver,

preserving the authority of his state, or it perishes. Unless in the heaven or the abyss there be one higher than Mannus, the dark thoughts of the Goth signify nothing. But none of them can be satisfied with the recognition of this hidden Being. There must be a manifestation of Him. From the immeasurable Time a Light must come forth, and that Light must be a Person. An Ormuzd must speak living words, nay, must be a living Word. Ammon must assume forms; the visible must, in some way set forth the invisible. One all clear and bright must be himself Wisdom to the Greeks—must utter the thoughts of wisdom, which keep them a people, and then must scatter himself through a thousand visible images. The Jove of the capitol cannot be only there. His presence must come forth in the host and in the family. Odin must travel lands, teach, give laws, and open Walhalla to men.

Look at each of these religions, and you see that there is a witness of oneness in all places and times. Look at them again, and you see there is something which divides them from each other. They feel that if they are to unite, it must be in something above themselves; they cannot unite for things beneath themselves, the accidents of their life, the climate, the soil of the lands in which they dwell, seem to determine what it is that is above them. They feel that if they are to unite, it must be in something above themselves; but their habits, tempers, tastes of their own minds, determine what it is which is above them.

This is the report which history gives of these religions—the mark which they have left of themselves in the actual universe. Dare you talk of all this as merely an illustration of the working of the religious principle in men? Dare you use such a dry, withered, heartless abstraction, to get rid of the recollection that you have been hearing how beings of your own flesh felt and did and suffered? Or can you comfort yourselves with saying, " These have all passed away; the Persian Ormuzd and Ahriman—the Egyptian dream of types in the world which must have some antitype—the Greek question, how is it I can create such marvels? what is it I cannot create?—the Roman sense of a divine order in the nation and family; the Odin warfare of good and evil spirits; they have passed away as visions of the night." Visions they were, but visions which came to men concerning the dreadful realities of their own existence. They were visions of the night, but by them men had to steer their vessels and shape their course; without them all would have been dark. And we belong to the same race with those men who had these visions; some were nearer to us, some more distant, some brought up in regions utterly unlike our own, some almost our kinsmen after the flesh; all our kinsmen in reality. It has not been a mistake, I believe, in

our education that we have busied ourselves so
much with the legends of Greece and Rome. If
we used them aright, they would not serve for the
food of an idle dilettantism—they would teach us
reverence and fear.   We should tremble as we
remembered ' These dreams of a beauty which eye
hath not seen, or ear heard, have visited the hearts
of human beings generations ago; the dark and
filthy imaginations which mingled with these dreams
were engendered in the same hearts: by one as
much as the other and by the fearful combination
we know that those hearts were like our own.
They will dwell together in us, and in time the
vile will seem real, the beautiful only a shadow,
unless we can find that the beauty has been somewhere substantiated ; unless we can see the beauty
apart from the corruption ; unless there is some
power which can establish the one, and destroy the
other, in ourselves.'

Such reflections often come, I trust, to the young
men of our land, as they read the classical fables.
Yet these belong rather to a refined cultivation, and
they may so possess the mind with the love of finite
forms as to make it forget that those who conceived
them could not be satisfied with them ; but craved
for the Infinite beyond.   It is otherwise with the
tales of our own proper ancestors. These are bound
up with the thoughts of our peasantry ; the most
ignorant man feels that they represent some of the
unspeakable fears and hopes of his spirit. And

9—2

they clothe themselves in no graceful forms. The storms and earthquakes of nature are the only adequate types of the conflict which they speak of, a conflict in which human beings of that day were actually engaged. Are we not engaged in it too? Have we asked ourselves whether we can bear up in it alone? if not, whether we know where help in it is to be found?

LECTURE V.

I SPOKE in my last Lecture of Mahometanism, Hindooism, and Buddhism, as the three great existing religions of the world; of the Persian, the Egyptian, the Greek, the Roman, and the Gothic, as the most conspicuous of those which belong to the past. It may strike some of you, that in one of these lists, though you may scarcely be able to say in which, there was a capital omission. Might not even the letter of Boyle's Will have reminded me, that the Christian missionary is likely to be encountered by Jews in all parts of the world? Is there any faith which has had a more memorable past than theirs?

It is indeed true, that a person must take a most imperfect view of society during the last 1800 years, who forgets that the Jew has had a place in it. Upon whatever age, upon whatever portion of the world he fixes his eye, this strange figure encounters him. He sees men without a place which they can call their own upon the earth, still feeling themselves to be *the* nation which has been chosen out of all others to be the head of the earth; men willingly submitting to the most grovelling occupations, and with a character seemingly conformed to these occupations, yet never

deserted by a vision, both of past and future glory;
men trampled upon by all people, and yet exercising a mighty influence, one which has increased
with the increase of riches and civilization, over the
counsels of statesmen and princes; men, who if
the time should come when no GOD but Mammon
is worshipped in the world, will carry a fearful
recollection into the very temples of Mammon of
a greater than he, who may be his destroyer. It
is true also that the Jew has never been without powerful arguments for that which he holds,
and against that which he denies. He can always appeal to his own consistency in support of
the first—to the persecutions and crimes of Pagans, Mahometans, and Christians, as evidence
in opposition to *them*. Though he cannot make
converts, though he does not wish it—for his
business is to keep the family of Abraham distinct from all others—he can do much to shake
the faith of those among whom he dwells. In all
times, of late years more especially, he has been
able to adapt himself to prevailing habits of thought
and feeling, to become conspicuous in art and
science, to enter into philosophical speculations,
and strangely to mingle the lessons which he has
received in the schools of the Prophets with the
wisdom of those who most despise them.

The Jew then may on these grounds be well
said to belong to the present, his religion to be
one of the existing religions of the earth. He
is a witness for something which is indestructible.

But he is also, by his own sad confession, a witness for something which is departed. If he or we can explain and reconcile these facts, we must turn to records which both of us profess to reverence. The question between us is, " What are the true principles of the old Jewish life and fellowship? in what way may they be most effectually asserted in our day?"

This, then, is my reason for not placing the Jew in either of those divisions to which I referred the other beliefs of mankind. We cannot go back in his case, as we did in the Mahometan, to the first promulgation of the faith, or, in the case of the Hindoo, to the earliest Vedas, without finding ourselves engaged in the assertion or defence of that which is as dear to us as it is to him; and we cannot interpret his present position, except by comparing it with our own. In following the course which I marked out for myself originally, we shall, I believe, be enabled to consider this subject from its right point of view. I proposed to enquire how the religions which have passed under our review stand severally related to Christianity. The first of these was the Mahometan. Now it is the Jewish side of Christianity in which we must seek for this relation. From the Old Testament we shall learn what are the great points of agreement between us and the Mahometan. In studying those points of agreement, we shall, perhaps, see more clearly the grounds of our difference both with the Mahometan and the modern Jew.

I. I endeavoured to shew you in my first Lecture that the mere dry, formal assertion of the unity of God, as an article of doctrine, was not that which had given Islamism its power. The proclamation, "There is one God," was no school formula; it was the announcement of a Living Being, acting, speaking, ruling. Now this is the leading characteristic of the Old Testament. Schoolmen giving you an account of it will say, that it is distinguished from all Pagan books by its assertion of the unity of the object of worship. But we have seen reason to think that this quality, taken alone, might not separate it from the early sacred writings of the Hindoos. Turn to the Book of Genesis or Exodus, and you at once feel the essential difference. There are no speculations about God, no questionings how man is to contemplate Him, or to be absorbed into His essence. He is creating the world according to a certain order; He is making man in His own image; He is placing man in a garden, fixing a certain prohibition for him, giving him a helpmeet, discovering his sin when he has broken the command, pronouncing a sentence upon him, promising him a blessing. He is punishing the murderer, visiting the earth with a flood, calling out a man to be a preserver of the race, sending forth his sons to people the earth, with the rainbow as a pledge of his mercy; scattering them abroad when they wished to build a tower, and to make themselves a name; calling a man out of his father's house,

and bidding him go into a land which should be
shown him, promising him that in him and in
his seed all the families of the earth should be
blest; giving him a covenant, giving him a son;
trying the faith of the father; revealing Himself
to Isaac and Jacob; guiding the Hebrew youth
into Egypt, causing him to bring his whole family
thither; hearing their cry when a king arose who
knew not Joseph, and made them slaves; revealing Himself to Moses as the I Am; sending signs
and judgments upon Pharaoh, bringing the people
out of Egypt, appointing them a feast in memorial
of their deliverance from generation to generation;
feeding them with manna, and causing the rock
to be struck when they were thirsty; proclaiming
the Law to them amidst thunders and lightnings;
prescribing the form of the tabernacle, and the
order of the priesthood; laying down the ordinary
rules which were suitable to them as an eastern
people; going before them in the ark of the covenant.

Nothing, you see, is set forth in the Hindoo
manner, as a dream, or thought, or reflection *about*
God; all is set forth as coming *from* Him; He
is, and He is doing. This is the Old Testament
language; this is the language which the Mahometan asserts must be true still. It is a record,
he said, but not merely a record—it tells us of
Him who was, and is, and is to come; of One by
whose command the world was made, and by whose
command it subsists; who rules and directs in

the affairs of men, not less now than of old. I
conceive that there is nothing in Christianity so
primary and fundamental as this belief; nothing
which it is so necessary for us to assert, in the
simple, practical language of the Old Testament,
and not to dilute by any modern phrases or unreal
substitutes. It was on this account especially that
I violated chronology, by considering Mahometanism before either of the other religions with
which it divides Asia; for I believed that it had
taken hold of the great first principle—that it had
begun at the beginning; not working its way up
to the divine ground from the earthly, but assuming that ground as its starting point. And,
at the same time, I wished you to feel how idle
the assertion is, that this doctrine merely belongs
to the world in its infancy; how when it seemed
to have become obsolete, amidst the arguments
and discussions of the schools, it stood forth again
as a living, terrific reality: as a truth which men
must be taught by the sword, if they would be
taught it in no other way.

II. Next, the Mahometan believed that the
Lord of All does actually make His will known
to men; that He speaks, and that they can hear
and obey His voice. This is the second most obvious characteristic of the Old Testament. Abram
is called out of his land by the unseen Lord. He
knows that he is, and he does what he is com-
manded. Moses is bidden to go in before Pharaoh;
he shrinks from the work, but he is certain that

the Lord God of Abraham and Isaac and Jacob
has sent him.   Thus Revelation, or the declaration
of God's mind and will—of God himself—to man,
is assumed as the ground of action, and history,
and knowledge.   It is not put as a vague, distant
possibility that such communications *may* be made
to man, that they may reach him; it is declared
that they must reach him, or that he is helpless
and ignorant.   He must act under a divine call
of some kind, or he cannot act rightly.   The Mahometan affirms that this truth of the old time is
a truth of the later time.   In the seventh century after Christ, Mahomet claims to be called
of God to a work.   We may believe that in many
points he greatly mistook the nature of this call,
of this work.   But the principle that any man
who rouses the heart of a nation, who proclaims
any deep truth in the midst of it, has a calling—
a calling from God—that he has no right to deny it
or to explain it away ; that he cannot do what
he is meant to do except on the faith of it ; this
is a conviction which we Christians have inherited, or ought to have inherited, from the Jew
quite as much as the Mahometan.   Our own language is framed upon the supposition : we speak
of callings and vocations.   If the words mean nothing, it is a great pity that we should use them.
It is lending ourselves to a falsehood—it is con-
tracting a false habit of mind.   But I am sure
they have meant something to men in past times—
to all good and great men, who have really served

their generation in any kind of work. And I
do trust and believe that they mean something
to some of us still ; that we feel we should be
parting with what is most precious, if they ceased
to mean that something—that we desire they should
mean much more.

III.   But, thirdly, the Mahometan, while he
acknowledges that the voice of God thus speaks
to men, believes as strongly that there is meant
to be some record of His utterances—some book of
which it may be said, This is *the* book. He cannot part with this conviction ; it is necessary to
him.   Whether or not he can explain how and
why the Koran should cease at a certain point,
he is sure that it was to cease at a certain point—
that there must be a Book which is complete, and
to which men may refer as an authority. The
Israelites, of whom we read in the Old Testament,
could not of course contemplate that Book as a
complete Book : it was growing. Their own lives
and histories were contributing to it. Their Patriarchs had no Book. Still, from the time that
the Law was delivered, they were convinced that
they had that written in enduring letters which
proceeded from God. They believed that His
communications were meant to be preserved in letters. They laboured to preserve them, and to
keep them apart from all which they believed was
not His. They had confidence that God Himself would watch over His own Revelation. Upon
us this conviction also has descended; we agree

with the Mahometan that the belief in a Book of
Revelation, a completed Book, is not incompatible
with the idea of God ruling in the world *now*—
of His calling men to do a work for Him now; nay,
that the one truth is necessary to the other. Why
Mahomet required a new Bible in the seventh century, why we do not require it, is a point to be
considered hereafter; that which I am pressing
here is, that both alike do feel the need of a
Bible—of a Divine Book.

IV. But the Mahometan does not only look
upon the peculiar Prophet as called of God. He
believes that the whole body of Islamites is a body
called by God to the work of proclaiming Him, and
putting down whatever sets itself in opposition to
Him. I need not remind you that the children
of Israel had this belief before them. In the
strength of it they went—a little handful of men,
who were lately Egyptian slaves, and drove out
the Canaanitish people; beating down their walls,
and slaying them with the edge of the sword.
They were not a wild, undisciplined host—a
terrific horde, like the Huns or the Avars of
later times; they were most orderly; divided according to tribes, each man encamping beside the
standard of the house of his fathers, marshalled
under regular leaders, practising the ordinary methods and stratagems of war. Still, that which
gave them all their energy, that which made them
one people, that which caused their discipline to
be an instrument of their valour, not a substitute

for it, was a belief that the Lord of Hosts was
among them, that they were His soldiers, and mov-
ing under His command. They were sure that
they had a commission from Him to punish a
people the cup of whose iniquities was full. They
were sure they were not doing a work for themselves, but were executing the purposes of His
Will. And this the Mahometan says is the true
law of armies, the right spirit for men of later
as well as earlier days, to fight in, and to act in, at
all times. They must feel that an Unseen Power
is in the midst of their host; that they are His
soldiers. We are often told that the opinion is a
mistaken and a dangerous one; one which belonged to Judaism, and which Christianity discounte-
nances. I cannot think so. That there is a sense
in which the disciples of the Koran have perverted
Jewish example, I shall endeavour to shew presently. Perhaps we shall find that the perversion
has been in not adhering to it closely enough. But
I do not think that any Christian nation has
ever been the worse for believing that it was acting
as the minister of God. Our forms and proclamations always express this. Have we been better
when these forms and proclamations were real and
significant, or when they were false? It seems to
me, that the more we come to think these phrases
not merely phrases, but the expressions of what
is true, the more simple and honest our lives will
be, and that when to any nation they become mere
phrases, its life, I need not say its Christianity,

is gone.   I feel very sure that the sense of a Divine
Presence has never utterly forsaken, and does not
forsake, any host of Christian men fighting by land
or sea : or that, if it do, their arms become palsied,
and they become the shame of their enemies.   They
may act very inconsistently with this profession ;
the inconsistency no doubt weakens the reality of
it ; but it is not a mere profession.   Asking the
help of God may be a poor formality to easy, luxu-
rious men ; those who are on the eve of battle,
who are standing between life and death, have no
time for words unless they mean something.   And
they have a signification as of old, otherwise a feeble
force would not be able to put a greater one to
flight, supported by all the advantages of position,
and the resources of art.   When our soldiers shall
utterly disbelieve that the same Lord who went
forth with Joshua and Gideon is with them, see
whether we shall not have tidings of cowardice and
ignominy, not of courage and triumph.

V.   We saw how much the office of the caliph
or sovereign had blended itself with Mahometan
life and history, how the visible centre of the
host recalled to each soldier the sense of his alle-
giance to Allah the Unseen King.   Here, again,
we are reminded of the Old Testament.   David,
and every true king, felt that he reigned by covenant with God, that he was the witness of Him
to the people.   And his people returned the feeling.
Looking up to Him, they felt that they were a
people indeed—it was not a dream ; they were so

actually; they had one heart, one with each other, one with those who had gone before them, one with those who should come after them. Of course such language is liable to misinterpretation. There were crimes and divisions in the times of David and Hezekiah, as at all times. Scripture does not conceal them, but declares them, and shows the punishment of them. When any evil deed was perpetrated by the king it destroyed the reverence of the people for him, and so their own unity. On the other hand, their evil condition re-acted upon him, and led him to depend more on the number of his armed men than upon the strength of Israel. These facts do not weaken the assertion I made, but illustrate it. Do not they seem also to prove that these records are not merely records of the past, or of a particular nation, but that they explain the bonds by which sovereign and subjects are connected according to a divine and immutable law, in all times and in all nations? So the Mahometan thought in his own case. Had the people among whom he came felt the same; had there been that real vital relation between the monarch and those who paid him homage, which there was between the caliph and the soldiers of the Crescent, those soldiers would not have triumphed as they did. This is no rash assertion; it is borne out by the experience of history. Asia was not able to resist the armies of the prophet, because there was no such national feeling as that which I have described. Constantinople could not ultimately resist them, for there was nothing like it in the Greek empire. They were resisted in Western Europe, for there a set of Christian nations had gradually grown up, believing, amidst many confusions and inconsistencies no doubt, but still practically believing, that their kings were covenant kings, reigning in the name of the Lord, as much as the kings of Judah had ever done.

These are some of the points of real affinity between Christianity and Mahometanism. I say *Christianity*; meaning thereby that though these principles belong to the Old Testament, and not to the New, as such, yet that Christians can adopt them and realize them, and that Jews, who seem to stand upon the ground of the Old Testament, cannot. I do not say this in reproach to them, I merely state it as a fact. All the most living principles of the Old Testament, those which were embodied in the life and history of the Jewish people, have become dead letters to their descendants. They retain the acknowledgment of the Divine unity as against anything which contradicts it, or seems to them to contradict it. But the sense of a Living Being, of One speaking, acting, ruling, this may dwell deep down in the heart of Jews; it may have been drawn out by persecution in many; but, so far as we can judge, it is always threatening to become dried up in a formula among the orthodox Israelites, to lose itself in pantheistical phrases among the liberal and intellectual. The former class will readily acknow-

ledge a Divine Book, but for the very purpose
of keeping out the notion of any real intercourse
between heaven and earth since it was closed.
And yet this Book will not satisfy them; it must
be stifled under Rabbinical interpretations; all its
practical, homely, awful realities, must be reduced
into notions, and speculations, and frivolities. The
liberal class will gladly avail themselves of phrases
about a living voice, that they may throw off
the burden of these interpretations, and in fact
of the Book which they oppress. But the living
voice does not proceed from a personal being who
has a right to command his creatures; there is no
bowing to it as to that which must not, cannot
be resisted; no acknowledgment of a high calling,
no feeling of a relation to the past; only a
claim to be independent, to think and feel differ-
ently from those who went before—a very natural
tendency, surely, in men who have been under a
grievous yoke, but offering little hope that they
will be emancipated from it, or will not fall under
a more grievous one still. Hence, it is not to be
wondered at that the reality of that which is
unseen, for which the Jewish worship bore such a
wonderful testimony, should be lost in that very
worship, that its ceremonial should bind the spirit
to earth instead of raising it. No wonder that the
most vulgar of all outward things, the mere coin
by help of which one is exchanged for another,
should have become the great object of heart de-
votion. To speak of this people as not having any

longer any sense of the relation of the people to
its Sovereign, would be a mockery—that heavy loss
is of course inevitable. It is far pleasanter, and
more wonderful, to remember that the sense of
a national existence, of a national calling, has,
through all these centuries of degradation, not forsaken them. It has been upheld by that glorious
hope of a Deliverer to come hereafter, which neither
the Rabbinism of one of their schools, nor the
Pantheism of another, has been able to extinguish.
They had been almost 600 years without a temple
or a capital, scorned and hated by all people, when
Mahomet arose; yet when he bade them join his
standard as the reviver of the true faith of their
fathers, as the asserter of the Lord Jehovah against
his enemies, they utterly refused the invitation. He
thought, and perhaps rightly, that they were too
degraded to understand the words which he spoke
to them, too little worshippers of Him whom their
Scriptures proclaimed, to believe that He could really
interfere in the affairs of the world. His first great
war, therefore, was directed against them. If they
yielded they were not crushed, still less converted.
The belief that they belonged to the true stock
of Abraham, and he at the best only to an ille-
gitimate offshoot from it, that they were children
of the promises, and he was not, sustained them.
Here was the one sure thing which they could hold
fast, a token that the lock of hair on the head of
Samson, shorn, blinded, and captive, might still

10—2

grow again. There was a reality and continuity
in the national feeling of the Jew which the Islamite felt he could not encounter. There was nothing,
or scarcely anything in him, which corresponded to
it. He acknowledged a sovereign, his empire was
to spread far and wide; but, except so far as the
caliph or representative of Mahomet was concerned,
it had no connexion with any feeling of family, or
even country. Mecca became indeed the shrine of
religious worship for all Mahometans; but the practical centre of Mahometan society was at one time
in Persia, at one time in Spain, at last in Turkey.
So that a system, in many respects like the Jewish,
was in this one directly opposed to it. The Jews had
grown from a family into a nation, and, so long as
they continued a nation, were the great witnesses
against all attempts at universal sovereignty. The
Mahometans, setting at nought family distinctions
and national distinctions, attempted to bind all
races and languages together, under the authority
of one man, the successor of the Prophet.

This is a remark of great importance with a
view to the subject in which we are now engaged.
I have shewn you that there are many points in
which Christianity and Mahometanism both claim
affinity with Judaism, as it was set forth in the
Old Testament. Now we are come to a point in
which they both separate from it. The Mahometan claims to be a universal religion; to set
up a universal society. The Gospel does so too.

The questions we have now to consider are, on what basis these universal societies respectively rest, and what is the relation between them.

I. We have seen that it is common to Judaism, to Mahometanism, to Christianity, that they assert the will of a living Being as the ground of all things, that they speak of Him as declaring Himself, as exercising a continual, not an occasional, government over men. This recognition of a Divine, personal, unseen Sovereignty; of One who is not sought out by men, but who seeks men; who calls them, and chooses them to do His work, is the strength of all three. Each one of them becomes helpless when this faith is lost, or is exchanged for any other. But if you look at the records of the Old Testament, you will be struck by nothing so much as this—that this Divine Being is continually said to be declaring His NAME to men. In other words, it is not the *fact* of His existence chiefly which He is teaching them to acknowledge, it is His character—what manner of Being He is. He calls upon them to obey a Will; but each act of obedience brings them into closer acquaintance with Him who gives the command.

II. Hence we are able to understand the calling of the Jewish prophet. We are expressly told that he is called to know this Name. The character of God reveals itself to him in the different circumstances of his own history, or his nation's history. He is taught that the evil which he is conscious of in himself, and which he sees in others,

comes from unlikeness to the perfect Being in whose
image he is created. He has but a glimpse of the
Divine purposes and character, but it is such a
glimpse as is suitable to his necessities and the
necessities of his time. It enables him to understand what he is, and what his nature is, without
God—what the blessing is of being called by
Him—what the end of his calling is; namely, to
make this Name known to his countrymen; to
bring it out in opposition to the evil which is
most prevailing among them.

III. And so too he understands, and is able
to set forth, the purpose of his nation's calling.
It, too, was to proclaim this righteous name—to
exhibit the conflict between God and all forms of
evil—to shew that righteousness is a reality, and
not a dream—that the government of the world
is based upon it—that wrong and oppression are
not meant to triumph—that the earth is not meant
to be a den of robbers.

IV. But such a Revelation as this, though
it may be handed down in enduring letters—though
it may become a possession for all generations,
could never merely be delivered to men as a book
of sentences or maxims; it must come forth in a
gradual history—a history of Divine acts and human acts.

The Revelation assumes that God is altogether
distinct from His creatures; it must enable us
to feel that He is distinct from them. It declares
that He has made man in His own image; it

must enable us to feel practically that this assertion also is true. It treats man as we find him,
full of wrong and evil; it treats man as capable
of the highest good—as unsatisfied till he attains
that good. We must learn how these two things
are practically compatible. It must be a book of
life, then, not merely of letters—a record of real
men, and real events. It must shew how the
Divine Will directed events, and disciplined men
for that perfect good, that knowledge of Himself,
which he had designed for them. It must shew
how He cultivates those faculties in His creature
which he has given; how He enables them to
overcome the darkness and evil in the midst of
which they are struggling.

V. These are very obvious characteristics of
the Jewish Revelation : its origin in a personal
Being; its recognition of a righteous Name; its
speaking of each class in the nation, and of the
whole nation, as called to declare that Name ;
its human, practical, and historical form. But
there is another characteristic as obvious. The
history is always pointing to a completion, and
that completion in a Person. The Prophets have
a vision of a King who shall be the manifestation
of God—the perfect image of Him—*the* Man—the
Deliverer of the called nation, the ruler of all
the nations : He who should establish righteousness, should open the unseen world, should unite
earth and heaven. For such an one, these prophets say, David and his line were the pre-

paration—he would really establish a universal
kingdom. Now Christians affirm that the ground
of universal society is the Revelation of this
King. This Son of God, they say, has been
manifested; He in whom this perfect Image dwelt;
He has exhibited that Image in the life and acts
of a man, in the poverty and death of a man:
He, as a man, has exercised dominion over the
powers of nature; as a man, wrestled with spiritual
evil; as a man, triumphed over death; as a man,
ascended to the right hand of God; He having so
united man to God, has sent down His Spirit to
dwell among men, that they might be one family,
and glorify the Father of All in Him. The universal kingdom, say they, must be a fatherly kingdom. The Lord of it must be a suffering man,
who is yet the Son of God. That which makes it
one, and enables men to acknowledge God as one,
must be a uniting, reconciling Spirit, who raises
them above the broken forms and shadows of earth—
above those material things, in which there is nothing but division, into the true unity, the perfect,
absolute Love.

This, according to the Christian's faith, being
the kingdom which is meant for all men, he must
believe that God Himself designs that it should
be made known to men; that all people should
be brought into it. Men now, as much as formerly,
must be commissioned servants of God for this end:
there must be distinct callings tending to the ac-
complishment of it. All who have been brought to

acknowledge the true King must have a share in the calling. But that particular work which was assigned to the Jewish nation, of putting down wrong and violence, of asserting justice and judgment, though it can never be obsolete, though each nation must be called upon in its own place and circumstances to fulfil it, cannot be the highest work of all. For He who did the highest work of all, did it by suffering, submission, sacrifice; the great triumph over the greatest evils was won in this way. Power manifested itself in weakness; He who was most meek, proved Himself to be most a King. He who most proved Himself to be Divine, did so by becoming one with the poorest and vilest. This was not a novelty in the history of the world; in a measure it had been shewn before, that what is greatest is best able to stoop; that what can most bear to be crushed, has most capacity of life; that each thing must die before it can attain its perfection. The whole history of the world, rightly read, would illustrate this lesson: above all, it had been illustrated by the prophets and holy men of the Old Testament: nay, those very exertions of national strength and energy, which seem to set this principle at nought, were themselves exhibitions of it. The glory of the Israelitish conquest of Canaan was this, that it was the triumph of weakness over strength, of infused spiritual might over the height of walls and the bulk of giants.

But though men had been learning this lesson

gradually, the time which fully brought it out,
which set at nought all pretensions of outward
strength to dominion, which shewed that the power
of God Himself must be exhibited through weakness and death, in order that it may be felt to
be the power of Love; this was of necessity the
beginning of a new era.   Henceforth surely every
new event of history would demonstrate this truth
afresh.   Whatever power was working in the world
must submit to this, or be broken by it.   The evidence might be various, complicated, often contradictory; but it would all tend to this point—it
would assert a Loving Will as the ground of all
things; that that Will had been fully manifested
to men in the person of a man, who delighted to
do it; that it can only accomplish its ends by
bringing the wills of men into subjection to itself.

Now Mahometanism formally sets at nought
this idea of a Divine and universal kingdom; treats
it as a mere imagination which outrages all simplicity.   It goes back to the one principle of God's
sovereignty; cares nothing for that gradual un-
folding of a Name through a history of living acts;
assumes that the Book is given as a complete
scheme of life to the prophet; affirms that it is
the commission of the faithful to diffuse the faith
in this Book, and in the fact of the Divine sovereignty through the world; for this purpose invests
its caliph or sovereign with absolute dominion.

In the seventh century after Christ, then, Maho-

met taught that the world was to begin its history
again ; but to begin it with no hope of a progress.
That principle, which had been the mere starting-
point of Jewish faith, the ground of what it was
learning for 1900 years, was to be the one, all-sufficing maxim of Mahometan life.   The Koran was
to make it the one all-sufficing maxim for generations.
Now it *was* so grand a thing to proclaim ; God IS :
it had been proved so necessary by the experience
of the Jews to repeat this lesson, not only in the
ears of those who had *not* recognized it, but of those
who had—of those who professed to be living in
the continual recognition of it ; that I would not
retract a word of what I said in my first Lecture
concerning the needfulness and the blessing of the
Mahometan witness, and of the terrific teaching by
which it was enforced.   The Jews who were so
ready then, and have been so ready at all times,
to make of their Testament only another Koran,
a book of notions and sentences, would thus be
reminded, if anything could remind them, of the
essential, eternal difference between the two, and
be led to ask " What *do* Old Testament records
mean, if they have their completion in themselves,
or if they have *not* their completion somewhere
else? what do they mean if, out of that family
and national kingdom of ours, some universal kingdom, utterly different from this, which the Mahometan is setting up, has not really grown ? "   And
the Christians were surely in equal, or in greater
want of an awful admonition to consider what they

meant by the words which they were speaking;
what substance there was in them. Why had
Mahomet supposed that a new Bible must be sent
from heaven more than five centuries after they
had declared that the Bible was closed? There
was no great new fact declared to mankind. So far
as it told them anything, it only repeated what
they knew before. The other, and main object
of it, was to deny that fact of the actual manifestation of God—of the actual union of God with
man, on which they professed to rest all their
hopes for themselves and for their race. But did
the Koran deny this fact more than they themselves had denied it? Were they acknowledging
the fact by merely disputing about it? Did it
mean anything to them? Was it not the clearest
proof of a Divine government over the world, that
they were not permitted to go on in this stupid
unreality—that they were taught, even in such a
method, that the words they admitted, must be
more than words, or, even as such, must be taken
from them?

Nor were the Mahometan conquests themselves
in the least degree confutations of the Christian
principle, that not outward strength, but weakness,
trusting in God, is the cause of ultimate success.
They were weak when they began. They triumphed, because they had more faith than their
adversaries. Even in the triumphs of the Crescent
there was a witness for the doctrine of the Cross;
and every new Christian saint and martyr who

learnt, in struggling against them, where help is to
be found in the time of need, every Christian nation
which learnt to confess Christ as its real King, and
in His might to resist the oppressor, found, and
proved to the world, that Mahometanism had not
weakened that truth, but had only made it more
manifest. Because the Mahometan recognizes a
mere Will governing all things, and that Will not
a loving Will, he is converted, as we saw that he
had been in the course of his history, from a noble
witness of a Personal Being into the worshipper
of a dead necessity. Because he will not admit that
there has been really a man in the world who was
one with God—a man who exercised power over
nature, and yet whose main glory consisted in
giving up himself, therefore he cannot really assert
the victory of man over visible things when he tries
most to do so. He glorifies the might of arms
when he most talks of the might of submission.
Because he does not acknowledge a loving will
acting upon men's wills, to humble them in themselves, and to raise them to God, therefore he
becomes the enslaver of his fellows, therefore cheer-
ful obedience to a master, which for a while distinguished him, becomes servitude to a tyrant. Because he will not acknowledge that the highest and
Divinest unity is that of love, but rests all upon the
mere unity of sovereignty, he has never been able to
establish one government upon the earth. Mightily
as he has fought for it, his kingdom has ever been
splitting into fragments ; one race has displaced

another; nations have broken loose from the recognized centre in each different age. It has been
found that such a universality or unity is merely
material; that it has no root in the nature of
things—in the Divine order; that each new age
must do something more to weaken its integrity
and hasten its dissolution.

Two questions, I hope, may have been partly
answered by these observations. The first is,
whether Christianity must abandon its claims to
be a Revelation, in order that it may deal fairly
with the Mahometan? The second, whether it
can strengthen and quicken that faith of his which
we found was so ready to perish? Whatever pre-
tends only to be a better system of notions, a
better scheme of conduct than his own, he will
reject while he has the courage and constancy of his
fathers; will only receive because he has sunk into a
state in which it is indifferent what he holds, or
rather, in which it is impossible for him with a real
vital grasp to hold anything. Mahomet was believed by those, and those only, who felt that he
brought a message from God; nothing which does
not come as a message from God can reach the
hearts of those who still acknowledge him. And of
what form must the message be? If it sets at
nought the first conditions of his original faith,
nay, of his very existence, this he is certain cannot be from God; yea, he knows it must be from the
devil. Only that which assumes this as its eternal
foundation, and which deepens and expands it so

that the facts of human life which seem least in
accordance with it shall be shown to rest upon
it, will carry that Divine stamp which the reason
and conscience it awakens will recognise. Therefore we agree with the arguments of our opponents
to this extent. Supposing they had proved the
Gospel not to be a revelation, but only a product
of the human intellect, their conclusion is incon-
testable. It ought not to be presented to the Mahometan ; it is utter folly, or else cruelty, to inflict
the proclamation upon him. But if it do not follow
from the likeness which has been detected between
Mahometanism, Judaism, and Christianity, that
they are all equally deceived in their great postulate;
if it appears that Christianity reveals that which
alone interprets that postulate, and prevents it
from sinking into a dead notion; then we have
found that power which can avenge the outrages
and injuries of Islamism, by preserving the precious
fragments of truth which are lodged within it,
forming them into a whole, making them effectual
for the blessing of all the lands over which it reigns.

And surely, if this be the way in which we can
and should speak to the Mahometan, no other can
befit us in our intercourse with the Jew. Whatever
there is in him of strength or earnestness clings to
the belief that God spake to his fathers. Systems,
rabbinical and philosophical, may choke that belief; money-getting habits may almost extinguish it.
But it haunts him; it is an oppression to him,
from which in these ways he seeks to be delivered

when he is in an evil state of mind; it is his only
consolation and hope when he rises into a higher
one. With it is connected that sense of nationality
which is even yet his noblest characteristic, however
mixed it may be with sin and weakness. To it is
linked that hope of a coming Deliverer which sometimes cheers him amidst all the misery and anguish
of his actual condition. A religion which is not a
message from God, not an unveiling of Him, is
at once felt by him to be a phantasy. He may
adopt the modern talk about the religious instinct
or principle creating its own object; but it is in
his mouth, if in no other person's, absolutely insincere. Again then we say, if Christianity be not
a Revelation, or we do not think it is, we are right
to keep it from the Jew, as being something with
which his mind can have no possible affinity. But
if it be this; if it be such a revelation as rests
upon his data, as justifies his nationality, as establishes his hope of a Deliverer, while it takes
from these convictions that narrowness which he is
beginning to find incompatible with his apprehensions respecting the condition and greatness of men;
shows how the nationality, without being lost, may
be expanded into a universal fellowship; hinders
the vision of a future revelation from degenerating
into the expectation of a sensual and mundane felicity, by declaring that the Redeemer has come already to claim Man for his possession, and to rescue
him from his earthly bondage; then we may feel in
this case that there is One power, and but One in the

world, which can raise the fallen Israelite to a
new and spiritual life.

There is, however, another view of the relations of Christianity with Judaism and Mahometanism—another, and a most important one. If
Christianity deserve that character in which I have
endeavoured to present it, it has, and it ought to
have, its Judaical and Mahometan side. It may,
as I have said, alienate this part of its own possession ; it may forget the great truth which it has
inherited from Judaism, the truth of a living King
and Lord of the World; it may try to sever the
doctrine of Christ from this absolute and eternal
ground; then that doctrine loses all its meaning,
becomes a shadow, and not a substance—a dogma,
not a living word. Then God does assuredly raise
up some witness for this truth, lest men should
be robbed of it.   But it is possible for Christians
to take another course, if it be another ; it is possible for them, apparently, to exalt the Judaical
or Mahometan side of Christianity, to become, in
fact, practically Jews or Mahometans, though they
do not belong to the family of Abraham, and
may care nothing about the Arabian Prophet. In
practice Christians have done this when they have
attempted to copy Jewish example in the manner
of propagating their faith : really copying not that,
but Mahometan example : for we truly copy Jewish example, as I have shewn you, when we go
forth as national bodies, under our national sovereign, to resist wrong and robbery, and to maintain

the position which God has given us: we copy
Mahometan example when we attempt to spread
the principles of the Universal Family, which is
based upon the Love of God, and the Sacrifice
of Christ, and the gift of the Spirit of meekness
and of charity, by any other methods than those
of love, and sacrifice, and meekness. We seem to
copy Jewish example—we really copy Mahometan
example, when we seek for any visible, mortal man
to reign over the Universal Family; for the Jewish
king reigned not over the universe, but over a particular nation: and so soon as a universal society
grew out of the national one, it was the glorious
proclamation that an Unseen King, who had ascended to the right hand of God, was its only
Sovereign. We seem to copy Jewish example—we
really copy Mahometan example, when we set visible
and outward rewards before us as the prizes of our
high calling; for though the Jew lived especially to
assert God's dominion over the earth, and to rule it,
and subdue it for Him, yet the reward he always
kept in sight was, that he might know Him who
exercised righteousness and judgment in the earth,
that he might awake up after His likeness, and be
satisfied with it. In like manner we copy the example of the modern Jew and of the Mahometan,
not of the ancient Jew, or if of the ancient Jew,
only of the formal, heartless Pharisee, when we receive the Bible not as a record of actual doings, of
actual intercourse between a living Being and His
creatures upon earth, but only as a collection of

notions and opinions, about which we are to dispute
and tear each other in pieces. Still more effectually
do we assume the character of the servant of the
Prophet, of the degenerate Israelite, when we set
up the dry confession of God's sovereignty against
his righteousness, supposing that His acts are ever
acts of self-will; that His glory is ever anything
but the glory of purity, and goodness, and truth.
In all these ways we may prove that there is indeed
a very near relation between our belief and theirs,
inasmuch as we can hold the one under the name
of the other.

Again, we may adopt what some would call,
I think wrongly, a merely theoretical Judaism, or
Mahometanism; we may seem to copy Jewish example by asserting the simplicity of God's nature;
by denying the possibility of a man manifesting
forth the Unseen God, by rejecting the belief of
a Father and a Son, and of a Spirit binding them
together in an ever-blessed Unity. Why this is
not the adoption of the true Judaical Faith, but
the rejection of it, I have explained already; it
has been ever ready to issue in the dryness of
modern Judaism wherein all which we see alive in
the Old Testament, is petrified. Now especially
that result is inevitable; for now, less than in any
former day, is it possible to speak of God as if he
stood in no relation to man. The tendency of
our time is to confound Him with His Creatures,
with the works of His hands; to lose all thought
of His distinctness; to regard Him as only the

conception of man's mind, a sort of synonyme for
man's thinking faculty, or for the life which dwells
in things. Against such notions the records of
Judaism and Mahometanism are mighty and standing protests; but they are more and more ineffectual
protests. They shew why such notions of God can
never satisfy human beings who know their own
necessities; not what these notions signify, and
how they are to be satisfied.

It is true, then, that the temptations of Jews
and Mahometans are our temptations; that we
carry their practical confusions and divisions within
our own bosoms. At every moment we are liable
to fall into them. Each careless step we take, each
unholy temper we indulge, the neglect of our duties,
the tolerance of our evil, is always increasing the
danger. It is true also that the Christian has
no right to undervalue any good thing which he
finds in any Jew or Mahometan; it flows from
a principle which he ought to hold fast, and which
ought to produce the same or better fruits in him.
While we acknowledge that every right act in
them deserves tenfold more admiration than it
could deserve in us, and that all our evil acts
must be done with ten-thousand-fold greater sense
of wrong and less of excuse, this confession does
not in the least affect that which we believe; for
Christianity is not concerned in justifying our
sins, but in condemning them : it does not say
that any particular set of men, calling themselves
by the Christian name, are better than others;

but it says that God will be true, though every
man be a liar; that his kingdom will be established
whether we who belong to it care that it should
be established, or cut ourselves off from it. And
the same conscience which tells us of our evil, forces
each of us to say: 'This evil comes not from my
faith, but from indifference to it. It comes not
from my holding too fast by that which is simple
and old rather than seeking for a new and finer
Christianity. It comes simply from my forgetting
the Creed of my childhood. For if I did believe
in God the Father Almighty, Maker of Heaven and
Earth, I should be acknowledging that Will which
Jews and Mahometans acknowledge as the ground
of all things: only I should be confessing it as
a loving and fatherly will. If I did believe in
Jesus Christ His only Son our Lord, who was
conceived by the Holy Ghost, born of the Virgin
Mary, suffered under Pontius Pilate, was crucified,
dead and buried, who descended into hell, and
rose again the third day from the dead, who ascended into heaven, and sitteth on the right hand
of God, the Father Almighty, who from thence shall
come to judge the quick and dead, I should feel
and understand that there is indeed a Man who
will reign over the world, and judge it as Jews
and Mahometans teach; but that this Man is
the Son of God and the Son of Man; one who
before he claimed our homage, submitted to our
curse, wrestled with death and overcame; who
has already set up his throne in the highest

region of all, and calls upon every voluntary creature in his heart and spirit to do Him homage.
If I did believe in the Holy Ghost, the Holy Ca-
tholic Church, the Communion of Saints, the For-
giveness of Sins, the Resurrection of the Body,
and the Life Everlasting, I should feel there was
a mighty, Divine Power working in us, to make
us more completely servants of a human king and
of the Divine Will, than Jews and Mahometans
have ever dreamed we could be : to make us members of a universal society, as Islamites wish us to
be; to make our bodies more triumphant over
death, more glorious than they have thought possible; but, besides this, to make us sons of God—
brethren with Him who is the Son of God—brethren
with those who have passed into another world,
who are perfectly freed from temptation and sin,
who have inherited not a sensual Paradise, but a
kingdom of righteousness, and peace, and love.'

LECTURE VI.

THE subject which I propose to consider in my present Lecture, is the relation between Christianity and Hindooism. That such a relation exists has been felt by most persons, different as their theories have been respecting the nature or the cause of it. Christian writers on Hindoo antiquities have spoken of various traditions, which they suppose must have been derived, originally, from Scripture narratives—upon various Hindoo doctrines which have an obvious resemblance to some which form part of the orthodox faith of Christendom. Infidel writers have been equally willing to notice these correspondences, and have turned them to their own account. If any part of the Hindoo theories about the origin of the world recals the Mosaic account of it, this is evidence to them that both were alike the work of some early, imperfect theorist, that neither has any claim to divine authority. If the similarity is of an historical kind, the notorious confusion of the Hindoo records throws new doubt upon the Jewish. If, again, the likeness be between the great mysteries of the Christian faith, and the more recondite Hindoo speculations, what, they ask, does this shew but that these mysteries are the result of certain trains of human thought, and have only been attributed to a higher origin, because our forefathers had not the same means as we have of tracing them out in the minds of those whom they considered ignorant and idolatrous as we do.

I do not wish to conceal any of these objections; I am rather anxious to put them forward at the outset of my enquiry, because they concern not so much the results to which it may lead, as the method in which it shall be pursued. It is no doubt true that Christian writers have often caught at external, superficial indications of a resemblance between their own faith and that of other men, and have strained evidence to shew how it must have been produced. And I am satisfied that every such attempt to make out a case by ingenious twisting of words or perversion of facts, is sorely punished. For the impression left upon our minds, supposing the conclusion completely established, would be no more than this ; that certain opinions of certain people upon matters of history, or upon questions of a very subtle and refined nature, had something to do with similar opinions existing among ourselves, and might, perhaps, have proceeded from the same source. But the mere theories which we find in the sacred books of different nations, either about the past state of the world, or the system of it now, though they are worthy of our study and reflection, as hints (not always the most important hints) towards understanding what is the radical principle of the

mind and belief of the race which adopts them,
are not themselves identical with that principle and
that belief. Now when this is the case with that
to which we compare the Christian doctrines, it is
far too likely that we shall begin to think of them
in the same way. They will appear to us also
notions and opinions about certain great subjects; *divine* notions and opinions we may call
them ; but a mere name will not change their
character : we shall not feel that they have to
do with our own life and being ; we shall regard
them as truths which we are to hold, not as truths
which are to hold us, which are to give us a standing ground for time and for eternity. I do not
wonder, then, nor am I altogether sorry, that those
who have put forward this view of the relations
between Hindooism and Christianity should have
been taught that their own weapons may be used
against them. Such discoveries, instead of shaking
our faith, may lead us to feel more diligently for
the foundation of it ; to ask whether other nations
have not given evidence that they too need such
a foundation ; whether they are not craving to be
told what it is.

In considering the relations between Mahometanism and Christianity, we did not satisfy ourselves with shewing that certain precepts of the
Koran corresponded to certain precepts of the Bible,
and that the one was wrong when it had departed
from the other. It seemed necessary to examine
whether the main principle of Mahometan life,

that which had given strength to its hosts when
they were most strong, be or be not embodied in
Christianity, and whether there or here it has
most vitality, and is most in harmony with other
principles equally important. If we could not find
that the great Mahometan truth was asserted more
distinctly, mightily, livingly in Christianity than
in Mahometanism, we did not feel that Christianity could ever be a substitute for Mahometanism. If that for which the Mahometans were
content to give up their lives, were merely a
formal proposition in our faith, we were sure we
could not sustain ourselves against them. If anything wherein we differed from them weakened
this principle, that was so much of evidence against
us. Nothing seemed sufficient to us but the discovery that the belief in an Absolute Living God,
actually ruling in the world, seeking men, not
first sought by them, which is the root of all their
convictions, is the root of ours; that Christianity
perishes even more completely than Mahometanism
when this truth is forgotten ; that this principle
has lost its power over the Mahometan mind, or
been changed into one of the most opposite character, just because it wants the support of other
kindred truths, which belong to the essence of
Christianity.

Precisely in the same manner I would deal
with the present subject. In my second Lecture
I considered what were the permanent characteristics of Hindooism, those which had survived in

all its changes, and made its different changes intelligible, those which had resisted all opposition, even from truths which seemed mightier than they, and from men who were braver and stronger than those who upheld them. I would now inquire whether these characteristics have their counterparts in Christianity; whether they enter into the substance of it, as they do into the substance of Hindooism; whether the difficulties and contradictions which we found had grown naturally out of these convictions, and yet had weakened and impaired them, belong also to our belief; whether in that belief these Hindoo truths are or are not reconciled with those with which they had seemed to stand in deadly hostility. I have said again and again, that I do not think we prove our confidence in the divinity of that which we confess by subjecting it to light tests, by arguing that this or that is not justly required of it. Whatever has been found necessary in the course of six thousand years' experience, we have a right to ask of that which offers itself as the faith for mankind. And I do not think that it ever has shrunk, or ever will shrink, from any demands of this kind that we make upon it.

The position of the Brahmin in reference to the rest of Hindoo society was that which seemed to us at once the most obvious outward mark of the system, and its essential characteristic. Here was the radical distinction between Hindooism and Mahometanism; here was the key to its connexion

with Buddhism, and to the divergence of the latter from it. The Greeks under Alexander had
seen that the Hindoo people were cast in the
Brahminical mould—they retain this mould under
the English government in this nineteenth century
after Christ. Whatever principle then be the ground
of the belief in the superiority of the Brahmin to
other men, can be no mere accident of Hindoo
belief, no mere notion or opinion in the sacred
books; it must belong to the innermost heart of
the race. This principle we found expressed in
that distinction between the twice-born man and
other men, which is the characteristical one of the
Menu code. All mere distinctions of occupation,
even the distinctions of the four original classes,
seemed to resolve themselves into this. This, therefore, had endured, though two of those classes had
disappeared, and though the whole caste system
had undergone great outward modifications. This
had continued universal amidst all its local varieties.
Nor was there much difficulty in ascertaining the
main elements of which this distinction consisted.
First of all, it stood on the conviction that there
is in man that which is meant to converse with an
Unseen Spiritual Being, that this is the vocation
of the highest, wisest man, of him who is properly *the* man, who is alone able to guide and rule
his fellows. Next, upon the consideration that this
is not the natural, ordinary state of men, that that
is an ignominious, degraded, animal state, out of
which whoever is raised, must be raised by different

acts of purification, acts which are to bring him into a relation more or less intimate with Brahm. Thirdly, we saw that the idea of hereditary succession became involved with this, that the twice-born men became a distinct family, to be preserved pure from generation to generation.

I repeat these observations in this place the more carefully, because I am anxious that you should not suppose I am attaching any force to a mere phrase like that of the twice-born man. This phrase instantly suggests to every Christian an idea with which all his life he has been familiar. Hence, it might lead us to one of those hasty analogies against which I have already warned you. A person thoughtfully and earnestly considering such a subject as this for a great practical purpose, will be suspicious of himself when he finds that he is noticing a verbal correspondence; he will be aware of the temptation to build an argument upon it, and will understand how very easily he may be deceived by a translation from another language, made by men who were formed in an English school of thought, and were, perhaps, glad to catch at a rendering which would bring a lively and well-known image before the mind of their readers. I am quite willing, therefore, to forget this expression altogether, or to adopt any other that an Oriental scholar shall give me as a substitute for it, which has no resemblance to our own sacred dialect. It is the thing, and not the word, I wish you to notice; the deep conviction which has wrought

itself into the mind of the Hindoo, and which has
gone along with him through every stage of his
history. Still more earnestly would I remind you
that it is not the words New Birth, or Second
Birth, which characterize Christianity, but the
meaning indicated by them. To realize that conviction, let us, as on the last occasion, look at the
context of the Scriptures, not confining ourselves to
the New Testament, but beginning with the open-
ing of Jewish history.

I. You will remember how we traced the
idea of a Divine call through the whole of that
history. I referred to it then for the purpose of
shewing how everything in our faith, as in the
Mahometan, rests upon the recognition of an act
on the part of God. But in that call was involved
the idea of distinction, of separation. Abraham is
called out of his father's house, he is set apart
to be the head of a peculiar family, and the whole
of that family have a sign of that separation appointed for them. When the nation is called out
of its Egyptian bondage, not only is this sign
carefully preserved; not only is every institution
expressly contrived to keep this people distinct
from other people; but within the nation itself
distinctions begin to be established. The priest
is called out to the special work of presenting sacrifices, a whole tribe is set apart to the service of
the tabernacle. They are carefully designated;
the anointing oil is poured upon their heads;
garments of honour and beauty are given them;

Holiness to the Lord is inscribed on the fore-
head of the high priest. The last fact shows you
how completely the idea not only of a separation
is involved in these appointments, but of a separation for the very purpose to which the Brahmin is devoted. The priest is dedicated to the
service of the Unseen Jehovah. He is to enter
into His presence; to hold awful converse with
Him. His separation, in fact, is never for an
instant spoken of as having another object than
this. A gross animal taste, a disposition to honour visible things and bow before them, is characteristic of men generally; the elect people are
taken from the surrounding nations, that they may
be emancipated from this slavish tendency. Yet
the Jew is reminded that he is liable to it like other
men; that he must be cut off from it; that he
must look upon himself as intended for intercourse
with that which the eye cannot tell him of. The
priest explains the end of the nation's existence. It
is expressly declared that the tribe of Levi is taken
instead of the firstborn of all the families of Israel.

Here you see one very clear indication of the
principle which Hindoo society embodies; and this
principle is not less characteristic of the later history
than of the earlier. True the people began in process of time to mix with the nations round about
them, and to adopt their habits. But the wise
man always warns them, and the fact proves, that
hereby they were destroying themselves. When

they forgot their covenant, when they no longer
looked upon themselves as a chosen, separated people; above all when their priests lost sight of their
own vocation, and the purpose of it, feebleness, division, subjection to their neighbours, followed of
course. The fact does not change in the least degree
from one generation to another. The only change
is in the increased knowledge which the Jews obtain
of the reason and ground of the fact. This progress is very remarkable. The prophets tell them
more and more distinctly, that they require to be
circumcised in heart; that the separation must not
be merely from surrounding people, but from an evil
and corruption in themselves; that if they remembered the covenant of their God, and clave to
Him, they would overcome not merely the Moab-
ites and Edomites, but a perverse, grovelling habit
of soul, which was the cause of their idolatry;
that if they forgot this covenant, they would sink
first under the yoke of their own inclinations, then
under that of Assyria or Babylon. The more you
read the Old Testament prophets the more you
will see that amidst all the various circumstances
which surround them, amidst all the different methods of instruction which they are taught to
adopt, this is their great burthen. But is there
not a change in the New Testament? Did not
our Lord destroy that separation which the teachers
of the old time had been so careful to establish? Did not his coming put Jews and Gentiles

on a level? We must not permit vague phrases of this kind to hide from us the fact that our Lord, so far from obliterating the principle for which the Jewish nation had testified, asserted it, established it, expressed it for the first time in all its clearness and fulness. That, He said, which is born of the flesh is flesh, and that which is born of the Spirit is Spirit. Except a man be born again he cannot see the kingdom of heaven. In this language he gathers up the very meaning of the old dispensation; shews us what a truth was involved in every part of it; how every part had been a preparation for the full revelation of this truth. His coming was, no doubt, to destroy the barrier between Jew and Gentile; but not till that barrier had been proved to have its justification in the very condition and being of man, in his relation to God and to the world. If there is a flesh in man, by obedience to which he becomes degraded, sensual, idolatrous, if he naturally is obedient to this flesh, and can only attain the rights of a spiritual creature, when the Lord of All raises him above his nature, above himself, then we can understand why a whole nation should have been called by its position in reference to other nations, by its own strength and weakness, righteousness and sins, by the experience of all its individual members, to set forth this mighty fact in which the eternal destinies of men must be involved. And this testimony we hold is not, and cannot be, obsolete. The Christian Church claims to be a

body of twice-born men; claims to be a witness
of that mighty privilege which men have of conversing with the Unseen and Infinite, as well as
a witness of the tendencies which there is in man
to be merely animal and sensual. The Christian
Church claims a set of ministers who shall represent
the spiritual glory and privileges of the whole body,
shall be instruments in overcoming the low and
grovelling propensities of its members. Here, then,
is a principle which is as characteristic of our faith
as it is of the Hindoo, which has scarcely moulded
Oriental society more than it has the society of
modern Europe.

II.   It is impossible to separate the belief in
the superiority of the Brahmin to other men,
from the belief in his relation to Brahm. Tech-
nically we may call one a political, the other a
theological idea; practically, the former may, for
a while, survive the latter. But in any serious
investigation of the grounds of the religious system
they must be contemplated as identical. Brahm
is Wisdom or Light; the Brahmin is the reflection
of this Wisdom or Light. Such a view of the divinity, and of the way in which man is related
to him, is found in different modifications among
all those people who are members of what is called
the Indo-Germanic stock, and, perhaps, in some
who do not belong to it. While creative Will,
Command, Sovereignty, Separation from man, are
the attributes of Him whom the Arabian proclaimed to be the one God, Persians, Greeks,

Goths, each recognized Intelligence, an Intelligence communicable to man, and quickly involving human worship, as the object of their reverence. But long before this reverence had taken any definite form among these people, hear how strongly it was expressed by those Hebrew sages who seemed to live for the assertion of the Mahometan truth: "I Wisdom dwell with Prudence, and find out knowledge of witty inventions. I am Understanding; I have strength. By me kings reign, and princes decree justice. By me princes rule, and nobles, and all the judges of the earth. The Lord possessed me in the beginning of His way, before His works of old. When there were no depths, I was brought forth; when there were no fountains abounding with water. Before the mountains were settled, before the hills was I brought forth: while as yet He had not made the earth, nor the fields, nor the highest part of the dust of the world. When He prepared the heavens, I was there: when He set a compass upon the face of the deep: when He established the clouds above: when He strengthened the fountains of the deep: when He gave to the sea his decree, that the waters should not pass His commandment: when He appointed the fountains of the earth: then I was by Him as one brought up with Him: and I was daily His delight, rejoicing always before Him; rejoicing in the habitable part of His earth; and my delights were with the sons of men."

Here we have the origin of the universe as-

12—2

cribed to Wisdom; kings and judges are said to
rule by Wisdom; Wisdom is said from the first
to have had her delight in the sons of men. Is
this an isolated passage; the dream of some particular writer, who had perhaps been instructed
by Chaldeans? On the contrary, it expresses the
very spirit of the Jewish economy, as it is presented to us in the writings of all its historians
and prophets. The wise king or the wise prophet
is ever spoken of in Scripture as having the divine
Wisdom, the divine Word with him, nay, in him.
He does not shrink from the pretension. In his
truest, humblest state of mind, he feels and confesses himself to be only a reflection of the divine
Light, an utterer of the divine Voice. He charges
it as a sin upon the false teachers, that they
only speak words out of their own hearts. Here
again, the New Testament takes up, expands, and
interprets the language of the Old. " In the beginning," says St. John, " was the Word. In Him
was Life, and the Life was the Light of men.
And the Light shineth in darkness, and the darkness comprehended it not." Of these words, and
of some which I have for the present omitted,
St. John's Gospel and his First Epistle are the ex-
position. They declare what this life was which
had been the light of men, how it was manifested,
who it was that could say, " I am the Light of
the World; he that followeth me shall not walk
in darkness."

III. But we detected a yet deeper conception

beneath that one of the relation of the Brahmin to
Brahma; we found that Brahma himself was supposed to be the expression or manifestation of Brahm,
who must be thought of only as Absolute, Self-
existent. These two ideas are inseparable. The
God is said to have sought for a companion of
his throne, and having considered and rejected all
animal natures, at last to have found his one
adequate image in man. This thought, often
strangely confounded, we saw was a pregnant one:
a dualism, not of opposition but of consort, might
be traced through the whole mythology.

Now, in the passage which I quoted from the
Book of the Proverbs, you cannot fail to have noted
the words, " The Lord possessed me in the beginning of his ways. I was with Him as one brought
up with Him." Beneath this Wisdom, this teacher
of the Sons of Men, this ruler of Princes, by whom
the sea and earth have been formed, there is
still a deeper and more unfathomable essence. Is
this a dream, mixing inconsistently with the rest
of the discourse? You cannot banish it without
destroying the sense of the context. Does it stand
apart from the general course and tenour of Jewish Revelation? You cannot understand the most
striking, turning points of that Revelation, if you
determine to pass by these words as incompre-
hensible or insignificant. Habitually the Jew believed that He whom he worshipped dwelt in
the thick darkness; no eye had seen Him; it was
unlawful to conceive any likeness of Him. But

he also believed that this Lord had revealed himself to Abraham, as he sat by the tent-door in
the heat of the day on the plain of Mamre; that
He had been the Captain of the Hosts of Israel;
that He had spoken to and by every holy seer.
Do you say, " These were difficulties, they look
like contradictions in the faith of this people ; they
seem fragments from different religions—witnesses
that they were not, as you pretend, the subjects of
a continuous, harmonious revelation?"   I admit the
difficulty ; I see why those who have never discovered it in themselves, should suppose it must
have arisen from the blending of two incompatible
traditions.   I admit, further, that the apparent contradiction could not be removed from the mind
of the Jew; that it must have haunted him—
sometimes have tormented him ; that the vision
of a reconciliation will only from time to time have
cheered him, in the fulfilment of lowly duties,
after hours of deep sorrow, in the temple-worship ;
that a verbal reconciliation could not satisfy him,
or any man.   But *a* reconciliation he and the
Hindoo both demand; the penalty of not finding
it is—Modern Judaism, or Modern Hindooism.   In
that passage, which I purposely mutilated when I
quoted it before, St. John says, " In the beginning
was the Word, and the Word was with God, and
the Word was God.   The same was in the beginning with God."   He states broadly, and in union,
the two truths which the former dispensation had
beheld separately, each of which had seemed at times

to stifle the other, each of which had again seemed
necessary to the other. But he does not attempt
to bring them together in words, until, as he believes, they had first been brought together in fact.
The Word, he says, was made flesh, and dwelt
among us, and we beheld his glory, the glory as
of the only-begotten of the Father, full of grace
and truth.

IV. I would beg you to remark how the Evan-
gelist speaks of Him here, first as a Word, then as
a Son. The Hindoo dreamed of Light proceeding
from a Fountain of Light; the Greek of a child
springing from a Father. Naturally, and without
effort, St. John recognizes both conceptions; for
the divine Wisdom is with him no abstraction;
the divine Son is with him no material image.
Hence there is no sudden transition from the divinest part of the Christian lore to that which
connects it with the popular faith of Hindooism.
The Word was made Flesh. A divine Incarnation is affirmed to be the great instrument for
redressing the evils of the world. It is declared
that He who had held converse with holy men in
their hearts, He whose life was the light of men
had brought himself nigh to all, so that he could
be seen with human eyes—handled with human
hands.

I have said that the Scripture speaks of *this*
Incarnation as the means for the redress of mortal
evils. But if we will use its language strictly,
we shall make a closer approximation to the Hin-

doo apprehension : we shall say that it was expressly to deliver men out of the power of the
Destroyer, to break in pieces his kingdom, that
the Eternal Word became one with his creatures.
Nowhere more distinctly than in Christian Theology is there the recognition of the fact which
the Siva worshipper perceives ; nowhere less effort
to make men comfortable by dissembling the fact,
that misery and death have gotten hold of the
earth ; nowhere a more emphatic affirmation of
the witness which the heart and consciences of
men have borne everywhere, but with special earnestness in Hindostan, that in them, in the region
of man's inner being, is the fiercest debate with
the evil which he sees without; that there, in that
region, he has to encounter it in its highest form,
in its most radical principle. The Gospel does
not start with a philosophical lie ; what man by
bitter experience has discovered to be his condition,
it assumes to be his condition.

V.   But dare we admit the genuineness of that
other page in the book of human experience which
the Siva worshippers would blot out?   The Incarnation answers this question ; affirms the Preserver
to be the Lord of all; affirms Him through the
whole course of His government to have been upholding this earth and those who dwelt upon it ;
to have been interfering for their rescue. Here,
in this very Incarnation, and that which follows
from it, is the assertion of his complete dominion ;
the answer to the Destroyer's claim to be in any

sense the Creator, to have any dominion whatsoever over that race which has paid him such fearful homage.

That which meets us first in the records of the life of the Son of Man upon earth, after He had been declared to be the Son of God, is a conflict, which no human eye could behold, with the Destroyer; next, the testimony which He gave outwardly of the truth He had in that secret battle made good, by delivering the bodies and spirits of men out of their bondage to inward miseries and inward tyrants. Yet never for an instant did.He speak of the claim which he put forth for the dominion of the Gracious Preserver and Father, as a new claim. Never when he spoke of setting up His Kingdom did he admit that He was not King of kings and Lord of lords before. The Jewish calling and economy had been asserting for generations the fact, that the Lord, the Lord God, merciful and gracious, slow to anger, and of great mercy, forgiving iniquity, transgressions, and sin, was the one Lord; that He had taken this nation to be His, to make them witnesses of His righteousness and government; that every one who received His Revelation of Himself, submitted to Him, and trusted in Him, was thereby brought into a righteous state, was thereby enabled to understand the purpose of His government, and to receive the blessings of it.

VI. Trust in this being lay at the foundation of the Jew's life. That trust involved Sacrifice.

They gave up themselves; so they rose out of the
dominion of that Spirit of self-will to which others
were paying homage; so they were able in their
daily acts to resist him, and defy him, and to
declare that neither in himself, nor in any of his
innumerable forms, images, apparitions, had he any
title to the obedience of God's servants.   The Jew
was taught that he was devoted, sacrificed to this
Lord, who had chosen his nation, and preserved it
from generation to generation, and who exercised
righteousness and judgment in all the earth.   It
was He who called the priest, appointed his vocation; to Him he was to bring the sacrifices for
himself and his nation; to Him, and to no visible
things; to Him, and to no unrighteous, hateful
power.   Sacrifice was the bond of the nation's existence; sacrifice the act by which man realized his
place in it, and came to understand its privileges.
The meaning, the law, the ground of sacrifice was
interpreting itself to the conscience and reason of
the true Israelite by every step of his discipline,
by every act of obedience, by his sin, by his repent-
ance.   More and more he felt it to be the law of
the universe; apart from which its very existence
is a contradiction; since only in perfect submission
to the perfect Will can any creature attain its life
and freedom.   He was prepared therefore for that
announcement which the Apostles of our Lord
made so boldly, that He who was the Son of the
Father, the Deliverer of Men, had offered himself
a perfect Sacrifice to God; that He had accom-

plished this act by entering into all the miseries of
man ; that with this loving, filial sacrifice, He who
was perfect Love was well pleased ; that in it was
the Atonement and Reconciliation of all Creation
to Him, in its original Head; that in the strength
of it each man might offer himself to God as a
reasonable, holy, acceptable Sacrifice.

I hope I have shewn in these last hints that
if the other portions of the faith of the Hindoos
have that which answers to them in ours, their
faith in the might and blessing of Sacrifice is one
in which we are bound with all our hearts to
participate. If there be any acts in past or present
ages on which we can think with delight, which
we can be sure had Christ's mark upon them, which
have wrought mightily, though in general secretly,
for the deliverance of men from idols, from intellectual or spiritual plagues, here has been the
root and spring of them. But it is just in the
point of deepest sympathy with this ancient people
that we arrive at the secret of our opposition. Upon
the question to *whom* the Sacrifice should be offered,
whether by it we propitiate a Siva, or surrender
ourselves in faith and trust to one who cares for
us and loves us; whether it is to overcome the re-
luctance of an enemy, or is the offering of our
own reluctant wills to a Father in the name of one
who has presented and is ever presenting His own
filial and completed Sacrifice—upon this issue, let us
understand it well, our controversy with Hindooism
turns.

The idea of a Kehama obtaining a power from his gods which they cannot afterwards resist, to curse and plague his fellow-men, is involved in the one doctrine, and is ready at any moment to come forth in a form of terrific wickedness, in the likeness of some Man-God. The Agony of the Garden, the spirit of the 22d Psalm, the Cross of Him who became nothing that the power, and grace, and Wisdom of God might through them shine forth upon all creatures; here we see the Christian Sacrifice, the Sacrifice of the God-Man. This Spirit of Sacrifice He promises to all who are made the Sons of God in Him. Everything then depends in our dealings with the Hindoos—let me add, everything in our dealings with ourselves— upon the degree in which we grasp this distinction, or lose sight of it. I shewed you that we are open to all Mahometan temptations. So are we to all Hindoo temptations. We may exalt a priestly caste, as if it were set up to make the rest of men Sudras; we may dwell upon the privilege of holding intercourse with the Divine Being, till we sink into self-worshippers; we may revenge ourselves for this abstract idolatry by plunging into outward idolatry; we may at last bow down before Siva, who we should have known was in all these ways drawing us into his worship, since every act of pride, spiritual, intellectual, sensual, is a mystery of his worship.

These dangers have discovered themselves in former periods of the world; seeing that they appertain to human nature, we may be as liable to them

as those who lived in any country or age. Is it
an escape from them to deny the existence of a
priesthood, to say that intercourse with heaven is
a dream, to scoff at all popular feelings, to maintain that the conscience of evil is nothing, that
sacrifices are a mockery? Or, rather to maintain
that a priesthood exists for the purpose of raising
men above animal degradation, as a witness of
the great rights of humanity; that, because intercourse with heaven was intended for the spirit of
man, and has been made possible for men, therefore lowliness and self-abasement are our most
proper and reasonable conditions; that poor and
rich, priests and Sudras, have been alike looked
upon, sympathized with, redeemed, raised to human
privileges by Him who took the nature of all; that
the man may be delivered from an evil conscience,
that he may renounce and scorn the authority of
the evil spirit, that he may offer himself in Christ's
name to God? This is the alternative for India
and for England. In other words, the question
is, whether we hold a system of opinions or a revelation from God? All Brahminical acts, services,
sacraments, imply an effort or scheme on the part
of the creature to raise himself to God. All
Christian acts, services, sacraments, imply that God
has sought for the creature that he might raise him
to Himself. The difference in our thoughts of
God, of the priest, of the sacrifice, all go back to
this primary difference. When we get into the
region of conceptions and speculations, all our views

of that which is divine will be fragmentary; some
of them will be very dark, because they are derived
from our own experience; either these become predominant, or in seeking to rid ourselves of them,
we deny facts and extinguish great portions of our
own being. To believe really, practically, that God
is light, and in Him is no darkness at all, we must
believe that He has caused this light to arise and
shine; we must seek to walk in it, and to see all
things in it.

In my second Lecture, I referred to the state of
the Britons, who had parted with their original
faith and had received Roman civilization, when
they were no longer protected by Roman arms.
I said the example was one which the statesmen
of British India would do well to ponder. To
abolish human sacrifices is good; but a blank will
be left in the nation's heart even by the loss of such
practices as those, which must be filled up, or we shall
impoverish those whom we seek to reform. But
there is another, sadder side of this history, one
which refers not to the conquered, but to the conquerors. Britain uttered her groan because Rome
could no longer send forth its legions. The hun-
dred hands which had been stretched from east to
west, from north to south, were palsied; for the
giant who moved them had become a child. And
whence came this decay of strength? All the signs
of it still belonged to Rome. From the city of
Jerusalem to the city of York she had traversed
the earth with her roads; within her own walls

were the mightiest trophies of art over nature. Her history told by what wonderful agencies human and natural, by how evidently divine an ordinance, her glory had been achieved. And to the gloss of civilization had been added the gloss of Christianity. The Emperor had believed when other help was failing, that in the might of the Cross he might still conquer. The sign was indeed there, but it was marked upon the standard, not written upon the hearts of those rulers of the world. They saw not what it meant; how it interpreted and crowned all that had been great in their history hitherto; how it separated the real great from the real little; how it sanctified all those feelings of obedience, duty, reverence for unseen law, self-devotion, by which the city had risen from nothing; how it poured contempt upon dominion, except as an instrument by which the highest might serve the lowest; upon glory, except as it grew out of humiliation, and was the exaltation of man above himself. The civilized Christian Roman had lost the heart, the reverence, the faith, which belonged to his rude Pagan ancestors; that Christianity and civilization might be victorious, the miserable patrons of both must be swept away.

If it be so with us; if our civilization merely consists in those outward conveniences and mechanical inventions which are the fruits of it, assuredly we shall impart but that which we have; we shall communicate only our external polish to the nations which we rule; their inward condition under

our hands will become less strong, less sound, than
it was before.   If our belief in Christianity floats
upon the surface of our minds, just keeps itself alive
by a few phrases and conventions in the multitude
of our pursuits; if it offers no greater evidence
of its vitality than the debates and controversies
which it engenders, assuredly we cannot present it
to the Hindoo with the slightest hope that he will
receive it in exchange for a faith which, be it good
or evil, has governed his life.   Only if our cultivation be of that kind which is truly human, which
delights to discern the essential humanity of each
nation, to honour it, to sympathise with it, shall we
understand that which is peculiar in our subjects, or
reform that which is corrupt in them.   Only if we
have received the Gospel as the answer from heaven to
inward perplexities which we have a thousand times
tried to stifle, but could not; only if we have learnt
that these perplexities are the groans of the human
spirit within us crying for deliverance; can we
with honest confidence speak to that spirit in
whatever region it dwells, in whatever language,
clear or inarticulate, it utters its voice, as one spake to
it of old, " Say not, Who shall ascend up into heaven?
that is, to bring Christ down; or, Who shall descend
into the deep? that is, to bring Christ again from
the dead : for lo! the word is nigh thee, in thy
mouth and in thy heart, even the word of faith
which we preach."

LECTURE VII.

THAT Buddha and Brahm are words of cognate if not of the same signification; that Buddhism is nevertheless essentially opposed to Brahminism, seeing that it denies the existence of a priestly caste; that the Buddhists are scattered over many lands, and have adopted various forms of belief and opinion; that their universal characteristic is reverence for the human intellect, which they think of as one, though diffused through many persons, and as having its central manifestation in the Lama; that Buddhism exists in China, beside two other forms of opinion with which it does not combine, I have explained in my third Lecture. It is now our business to inquire whether this system has any or what affinities with Christianity. If the inquiry is conducted fairly, it must satisfy these conditions. The resemblance which we detect, must be not in the superficial accidental parts of either faith, but in their radical and essential characteristics; these must not be assumed by the inquirer on his own authority, but must have some clear voucher that they are recognised as radical and essential characteristics by Buddhists and Christians respectively; the likeness must not be in that side of Buddhism in which it coincides

with Hindooism, otherwise we shall only be repeating
the last Lecture, but in that which is opposed to it.

The festival of Whitsuntide is observed in all
parts of Christendom; here in England, among
the Protestants in the north of Europe, by the
Romanists in the south, by Greeks and Armenians,
by the descendants of English, French, Spanish,
settlers in North and South America. It is felt
by all these to commemorate a great event, the
event which marks the establishment of the Christian Church in the world. They derive their notion
of this event from the record of it in the second
chapter of the Acts of the Apostles. There we are
told, that on a certain day which had long been
kept as a festival day among the Jews, numbers of
them were gathered from various countries of Asia,
Africa, and Europe, in the city of Jerusalem. In
that city dwelt a body of priests, divinely called, as
its inhabitants believed, to this office, members of a
priestly family. There were also authorised doctors
or interpreters of the law, whose words were received
by the great mass of the people as oracles. On the
day of Pentecost, says the writer of the Acts, a great
body of the inhabitants of the city, of the strangers
from other lands, were drawn to a place near the
temple, because they were told that a set of men, not
priests, not doctors of the law, but inhabitants of the
most despised part of Palestine, themselves of the
lowest caste, Galilean fishermen, were speaking in
different tongues the wonderful works of God.
This power the Scripture declares was given them

from on high. The Spirit of God had descended
upon them ; they spake with other tongues as the
Spirit gave them utterance. To the body thus
endued it is said a multitude joined themselves.
They were regarded with more and more jealousy
by the priests and doctors of the Jews. But they
spread themselves through Palestine ; they went
into other lands. Everywhere, they declared
that they came in the power of the Spirit, who had
thus broken down the barriers of language and
national distinction ; everywhere they said that this
Spirit would be given to those who believed their
message.

Are we to conclude from this story that the
Christian faith broke loose from the Jewish faith,
as Buddhism broke loose from Brahminism ; that
in each case there was a vehement reaction against
caste narrowness and local boundaries ; that in each
case this reaction was associated with the recognition of a spirit dwelling in men ? There may be
much plausibility in such a notion ; for many reasons
it would commend itself to certain modern philosophers. Only they would say, 'In order to make out
this resemblance, it is necessary to divest the scriptural story of its halo of mystery and marvel. Take
it as it stands, and all you learn from it is, that on
a certain occasion a particular miracle was per-
formed, unlike any that had previously occurred, or
was to occur again, at variance with the constitution
of man and the dealings of his Creator. In that
form it offers only a seeming analogy between the

13—2

Christian and the Buddhist doctrine; seeing that
the latter assumes the presence of a divine and
diffusive spirit to be the proper characteristic of
humanity, at least, in its noblest state, and that
on this ground it oversets the caste principle, not
for a particular emergency, but altogether. If,
however, you are inclined to admit that this is
merely the narrative of a remarkable epoch in
Jewish history (and indeed, in the world's history)
when there was awakened in the nation, or in a part
of it, the consciousness, previously slumbering, of
a capacity in men generally for that knowledge
which had been confined to the priests; a narrative surrounded, as all Hebrew narratives are, with
a divine machinery, we will admit that you have
established your case.'

I submit that one part of this statement is quite
incorrect. If I take the narration literally, I shall
not merely be told, that a certain event hap-
pened at a certain time and in a certain place;
I shall be told that this event was the fulfilment
of a promise made to the fathers of the Jewish
nation; I shall be told that it was intended for
those of that generation, and for their children.
These assertions, it will be remembered, are very
prominent in the discourse which the writer of
the Acts of the Apostles attributes to St. Peter.
One therefore who believes this statement cannot
look upon this descent of the Spirit, with all
that was implied in the circumstances of it, as
violating the laws of the human constitution, as

an exception in the plan of its Creator. He must look upon it as expounding that constitution, as carrying out that plan. But on what grounds, it will be asked, can it be alleged that the principles set forth in the Jewish scriptures and the Jewish economy were asserted and realised by a transaction which seems to destroy the exclusive hierarchy, ultimately the exclusive national limitation, which lie at the root of them? The answer to this question, will I believe, shew that the affinities of Christianity with Buddhism are much closer and more extensive than they would be on the hypothesis of the former being a rebellion against Judaism; on the other hand, will explain wherein the difference between them consists, and what that 'miraculous halo' which is imputed to the Scripture narrative, has to do with it.

We turn to the earliest of the Jewish records, and we find it declared that God made man in his own image, and gave him dominion over all the other creatures he had formed. Before a word has been said about the difference of one people from another, here is a broad fundamental assertion respecting man as man. Perhaps you will say, ' Yes; but this is set at nought by one which immediately follows it; the fall of Adam is the real, though the creation of man may be the nominal, beginning of the history.' As we are examining these records to find what they actually affirm, I consider the simplest, nay, the only honest, method is to take them, as beginning where they seem to

begin, not to assume a starting-point of our own.
It will then be seen more clearly whether they
have a connexion with each other, or are only
a collection of Sibylline leaves; whereas, if we
insist that the Divine drama opens at a certain
chapter, and that all which precedes is prologue,
we do not *find* the connexion, but make it. There
may be excuses in the arguments of divines for
such violence upon the text; but I do not think
it is ever justified by the conscience of simple and
devout Christians. I believe they would be shocked
to the last degree if you insisted in plain language
upon their believing that the constitution of God
was nullified, destroyed, or even at all affected, by
the evil acts of man. Undoubtedly, there is the
fullest, most immediate recognition of the fact that
evil entered into the world. There is no tampering
with experience, no attempt to represent the universe as something else than it is, in order to make
it accord with the account of its origin. There is
no hint of a golden age, during which sin and
death were not upon the earth. We are told that
the very first man forgot that he was made in
the image of God; yielded to the temptation of an
inferior creature; came under death. He denied
the law after which he was created. And each
of his descendants is shewn to have the same propensity to obey that which he was meant to rule ;
to disbelieve in Him whom he was meant to obey.
But neither the first man nor any of his successors
could make this degradation and disobedience any-

thing else than an anomaly and a contradiction. The worst man in Scripture is never represented as evil in any other sense than because he fights against the law under which he exists, and of which his very transgression is the continual witness. And therefore in the Bible God is ever represented as addressing Himself to the creature whom He had formed, as awakening in him by that voice a consciousness of his right condition.

He is represented as speaking thus to Adam when he was hiding himself from His presence; as speaking thus to Cain when he was meditating his crime, and when he had committed it. In each case it is assumed that the creature addressed stood in a direct relation to the Creator, however he might be denying it, and determining to shut himself out from it. And I need scarcely remind you, that he is treated, after the fall, as well as before it, as still intended to have dominion over the earth, and the animals upon it. The ground is cursed for his sake: in the sweat of his brow he must till it; but he does till it—he does subdue it. He is continually disposed to treat it as his master, but he is compelled to act as if it were his slave—compelled at the same time to remember that its power of producing nourishment for him depends not upon himself, but upon an Unseen Will, which he is ever inclined to lose sight of. The punishment of the race when lust and violence had spread over it. the preservation of it in a family, the blessing under which the sons of Noah

go forth to replenish the earth and to subdue it,
the confusion of their purpose of dwelling together
in one plain, when they were meant to people the
earth, bear witness to the same principle, Man, the
race of Man is treated as formed in the image of
God, as intended for rule over the creatures.

Now if this be the case with respect to the
records of the period preceding the Call of Abraham, those which follow can only be understood
on the same principle. The history of the chosen
people does not record an outrage upon mankind
for the sake of one portion of it; it is the history of men taken out of darkness into the light,
made conscious of their own state, as created in the
image of God and meant to have dominion over
the earth. A Mesopotamian shepherd is called
the friend of God—in him all the families of the
earth are to be blessed Out of his family grows
a nation. It is a witness to all nations against
the separate idolatrous worship which is dividing
them. Its members are taught to believe that
God Himself is their King—the Unseen God of
all the earth. They are not in some unnatural condition because they are taken under His government; their lives are simple, natural, orderly, in
proportion as they remember it; confused and irre-
gular when they forget it. As the history of the
nation goes on, there are continually new discoveries of evil tendencies, of an evil nature in
the members of it. They are not different from
the rest of the world ; they are equally idolatrous,

equally selfish, equally corrupt. Where then is
their advantage? The Lord of All has revealed
Himself to them; He has taken them into covenant; they may trust Him. In trusting Him they
rise above these selfish and idolatrous tendencies—
they become truly men. The Jewish Prophet,
when he is most overwhelmed with his own evil
and with the evil of his nation, obtains most apprehension of the truth that God will exhibit his
perfect Image to men, in a Man, and will so confound all the images they have made. Except
such an Image were really presented to them in
a Man—except it were really shewn to be true
that Man was made in the Image of God, and
had dominion over the creatures, and that Death
and Evil were not his masters, the visions of Jewish
seers were delusions. But St. Peter, when he spoke
to the Jews on the day of Pentecost, was firmly
assured that a Man had appeared in the world
who was the perfect Image of the Unseen God.
He believed that this Person had been declared
in the waters of baptism to be the Son of God;
that the Spirit of God had descended upon Him;
that in the strength of that Spirit he had exercised dominion over the powers of nature, over man's
spiritual enemies; had passed through death, had
ascended to the right hand of His Father. That
He should give His Spirit to men, to make them
the sons of God in Him; to restore them to
God's Image; to give them power over the earth;
to constitute them the masters, and not the sub-

jects of visible things;—this seemed to him the
right and reasonable fulfilment of express promises
which were contained in the Jewish Scriptures,
and of all their meaning.

With equal certainty he said, that the promise
would be to them and to their children. He was
sure that the Spirit of God had taken possession
of the powers, and energies, and speech of men.
He was sure that in yielding to that Spirit he
was obeying no strange, unnatural impulse, but
was yielding to his proper guide and teacher, to
the Author of all order, and peace, and unity.
More than this, perhaps, he may not have perceived.
To see in this gift the witness for a great human
fellowship; to see all that it implied respecting
man's creation and his redemption, was perhaps re-
served, more perfectly, for another Apostle. Through
intense personal humiliation and suffering did
the Apostle Paul learn that Christ by His death,
and resurrection, and ascension, had justified man
before God; that the Spirit of God was given,
not only as the fulfilment of all promises which
had been made to the fathers of the Jewish nation,
but as the fulfilment of the original law of his creation, when He made all things in Christ Jesus,
with the intent of finally gathering them all together in Him. In his Epistles we find him brought
into contact with men of different habits, philo-
sophies, and educations. The old mythologies had
prepared them very readily to recognise an inspiration from God. The sages very readily recognised

the worth of the individual soul in man; but the inspiration which the first admitted was sudden and casual, the honour which the other paid to the soul was solitary, exclusive, self-exalting. He spoke of a Spirit of God as given to dwell continually in man; to be the source in him of all knowledge, faith, love; the strength for all ordinary toils, the comforter in all sorrows, the power of exploring the unseen and the future. He spoke of this Spirit as calling forth a spirit in man, in the individual man, which lifts him above himself, which he cannot call his own, which belongs to him as the child of God, the member of a universal family—"the spirit of a man which is in him."

That profound feeling of reverence for the human spirit, then, which we have discovered in the Buddhist, his belief in the mighty capacities of this spirit, his determination to recognise these capacities as belonging to the race, not to some one section or class of it, his assurance that the spirit in man cannot be circumscribed by the limits of time or space, or by the measures and conditions of individual feeling and consciousness, his conviction that this human spirit must, in some mysterious manner, be divine, has its full justification in Christianity. And every subordinate idea which has grown out of these in the mind of the Buddhist has that which answers to it in the Gospel. He believes that it is the privilege of the divine man to contemplate the Divinity in His

purity. The highest view which St. Paul takes of
the powers of Christian men, in consequence of the
gift which had been bestowed upon them, is that
they might know God ; his most earnest prayer,
that they might increase in this knowledge. The
Buddhist believes that, in order to the attainment
of such knowledge, the mind must be separated
from outward, sensual things. Sanctification, the
deliverance of the heart and mind from earthly,
temporal things, that they may enter into the
enjoyment of that which is unseen and eternal,
is the very work which the writers of the New
Testament, with one accord, attribute to the Holy
Spirit who had been given them. The Buddhist
however, feeling that he must, in some way,
study the universe, and account for the facts
which he observes in it, was led to perceive the
necessity of a power which originates or begets,
a capacity which receives, a bond which unites
them. The Scriptures, too, suppose a power which
creates, a power in the creature which receives ; the
Scriptures contemplate the union and co-working
of these powers as the condition of health in
all that exists ; they shew how all destruction in
the human, voluntary creature has come from his
will not yielding itself to the divine, creating, inspiring Will ; how all restoration comes from their
being again brought into accordance. They speak
of the deepest ground of all things being the
awful union of the Father with the Son in the
Spirit.

Again, we heard of holy men appearing as benefactors of different portions of the globe; their footsteps traced upon earth, yet their home seeming to be somewhere else. What they are is known chiefly by what they have done; their acts are palpable; a mystery hangs about themselves. They are called Buddhas; though they appear in places and times far apart, the same wisdom, the same power dwells in them all; they must be the wisdom and power of Buddha; they can belong to no other. Even thus do Christians speak of those who in far-off ages, in various latitudes, have shed light into the hearts of men, have cheered the poor in the midst of their sore trials with help for the present, hope for the future; have restrained triumphant evil, and laboured that righteousness and truth might flourish. These we hold to be all partakers of the self-same Spirit; in their words and acts they manifest its presence; care not to be great in themselves, but do homage to a mysterious Greatness, from which all that seems such in themselves is derived; shew that they have their work on earth, their citizenship in the heavens. Once more, the Buddhist affirms that there must be some person, and that a human person, in whom the perfect wisdom resides. He need not in his earthly appearance be glorious; he may wear the form of a child, but the Power must be within, and must so reveal itself that men shall see the Divine Priest is there. Even thus is it the clearest, most invariable proclamation in

the Gospel, that each man, in his best, purest
estate, does but utter some portion of the Divine
Mind, does but exhibit some one partial image
of the Divine Character ; that there is one perfect
Utterance of that voice, one perfect Image of that
substance, one in whom the Fulness pleased to
dwell, one who humbled himself to the cradle of
Bethlehem, to the Cross of Calvary ; who in that
cradle, and on that Cross, shewed forth the Divine
glory : and who, because he humbled Himself, has
been exalted to be the High Priest of our race for
ever.

But as we have seen this relation between
Buddhism and Christianity coming out before us
with increasing brightness, we must, I think, have
become also more and more conscious of *some* difference, which, whatever it be, is a deep and radical
one. The philosophical objectors told us that if
we could separate the story of Pentecost from its
'mythical' accidents, the sound of the rushing mighty
wind, the cloven tongues, the notion of a particular
endowment bestowed by Jesus Christ at that particular moment on His disciples, we should arrive
at an intelligible result, which might throw some
light upon Buddhist and other history. I com-
plained of this statement so far as it represents
the events of that day as isolated, as inconsistent
with principles recognised in the Jewish economy,
as importing that the indwelling of a Spirit in
man is not implied in his original constitution.
Subject to these remarks, I now admit that they are

right in looking upon these miraculous circumstances as indicative of the difference between the
Scriptural and the Buddhist conception of the
spiritual endowments of human creatures. The
Buddhist starts from the human ground ; assumes
the existence or possibility of certain qualities and
attributes of a divine nature in man ; supposes the
man, in virtue of these, to hold intercourse with the
divinity. The Scripture starts from the divine
ground ; assumes that man according to his constitution is nothing but an image; denies that he can
originate anything ; sets forth a revelation of His
Creator to him as the foundation of his knowledge
of his life ; represents all faculties, powers, energies
of the creature as gifts of the Creator. Upon this
difference every other depends. If the first view
be the right one, there can, of course, be no divine
manifestation, for there is nothing to manifest.
The Creator does not witness to men by visible
signs that He is the Author of these gifts, for He
is not the Author of them, or He does not design
to make them know that He is. If the other view
be true, these (so-called) miracles, these exercises of
power, these signs of a Presence, are precisely the
methods which commend themselves to the conscience and reason of mankind as the most fitted—
I had nearly said as the only possible—witnesses of
a truth, which, when it has been once testified of in
this way, can hereafter be held as certain and
abiding though there be no signs of it at all.

Now, as Buddhism and Christianity are the

respective exemplifications of these two methods,
it may be well to compare the practical results of
each. You will see, I trust, my object. I do not
desire to make out a charge against Buddhism on
the ground of its moral deficiencies ; but, I want to
ascertain how far these deficiencies are or are not
owing to this characteristical feature of it, that
more than any other system the world has ever
seen, it makes the belief of a Divine power working
in man its ground, and ascends from that ground to
any apprehension it may entertain respecting the
divinity Himself.

I. One leading contrast offers itself instantly to
our notice. The Buddhist believes that a Divine
wisdom and power dwells, or may dwell, in human
beings, and that its dwelling constitutes them exalted, heroic spirits—saintly men. The New Testament begins with teaching us *what* kind of Spirit
this must be; what manner of Being He is from
whom this Spirit proceeds; what must be the
manner of His working in creatures who submit
to His government. It speaks of the Spirit of
Him who had declared Himself for ages to the
Jews as the God of Truth and Righteousness; it
speaks of the Spirit of Him who gave His Son for
men. It sets forth the character of this Spirit
by His life, in whom it is said to have dwelt without measure. If Holiness was more characteristic
of Him than power, the Spirit of holiness is the
name by which we are taught to express it most
uniformly and perfectly. If meekness, humility,

gentleness, were the essential qualities of His life, the Spirit is known as the Spirit of meekness, humility, gentleness: these are declared to be the fruits of its operations. If His whole life was an act of self-sacrifice, His Spirit is set forth as the power whereby man is able to offer himself a sacrifice. If love was the spring and end of His sacrifice, it is the Spirit of Love which He promises to those who obey Him. Not that these assertions in the least interfere with that other equally prominent one, which declares Him to be the Spirit of Truth and Knowledge; which speaks of all powers and exercises of mind, and all the directions which are given to them as from Him. No one brings out that assertion more clearly and mightily than St. Paul; but he winds up the enumeration of all gifts and powers in these words: "And yet I shew you a more excellent way. Though I speak with the tongues of men and of angels, and have not charity, I am become as a sounding brass, or a tinkling cymbal." Love is in his teaching, as in his life, the highest manifestation of the presence of the Spirit, because God, from whom it proceeds, is Love.

All this difference, you see, is grounded upon the difference between the naked idea of a Spirit dwelling in man and identical with himself, and that representation of Him as given to men by the Eternal God through His Son. Look now at the difference as to another point, the estimate of human creatures. To the Buddhist those whom he

believes thus endowed necessarily become gods, they
can be nothing else. And thus, he who starts with
throwing off an hereditary priesthood as an intolerable yoke, because men, as men, have the
capacity of seeing God and worshipping Him, becomes the poor servant and tool of a priesthood.
All who can exhibit the intellectual power which
he half feels is meant for himself, and yet which
he is conscious does not belong to him, must be
objects of his obedience and his worship. He has
no standard with which he can compare what they
are and what they do; he is sure that intercourse
with the unseen world must be a privilege of men,
that there must be some who exercise it; they cannot tell him what the exercise means, what the
result of it is, how he can be the better for it. They
seem to say, some of them actually say, and wish
him to understand that, at all events, they are
marking out a *ne plus ultra* to *his* enquiries, "Beyond us lies a void of Nothingness." Into that void
the listening disciple has no temptation to enter.
Yet he must satisfy his craving for the Infinite.
What can he do but accept these finite temporary
priests as the best substitutes for that which he
cannot obtain? They at least keep alive the appetite, they save him from utter despair. Such is
the condition of those who can only contemplate the
Spirit which they rightly feel is meant for man
as in man. The Christian is taught that he is
to think of this Spirit as *in* God, as coming forth
from Him. He is taught that he may ask God

continually for the quickening and renewing of it
in himself, and in all the family to which he belongs. He is told that when the Comforter comes
He shall convince the world of Sin, of Righteousness, of Judgment; that He shall not become identical with the man himself; but shall shew him his
evil; shall raise him out of that evil into a Righteousness which is above him, which is in one who
is gone to the Father; shall give him the continual assurance of a final separation between that
which is true and that which is false within him.

Thus the promise of the Spirit is the promise
of an ever clearer and growing perception of distinctions, of a power to overlook our own mind,
to judge its acts and movements, to know what
in it requires to be cut off, what is wrought in God.
Every human heart is to be the subject of it;
no creature that carries evil within it and belongs
to the race for which Christ died, is meant to be
defrauded of this mighty illumination. But no one
who receives it can pretend to be thereby exalted
above his fellows; his knowledge is the knowledge
of his own individual abasement; of that glory
which he shares with his race in Christ. And therefore the Scripture, in strict conformity with this
idea, represents all intellectual gifts as bestowed,
not to raise one man above another, but simply,
that men may be enabled to serve each other.
The Highest of All is the servant of all. He who
holds his gifts under this condition, and confesses
his unfitness for the use of them, is a fellow-worker

with the Divine Spirit. He is doing that which
he was sent here to do. He who uses them for
any other end, holds them on any other condition,
practically disowns the blessing which has been
granted to him, and its Author. The priest and
the prophet come especially under this rule. They
especially are to look upon themselves as called by
Him who came to deliver men out of their confusions and darkness, to an office under Him, as
endowed with powers by Him to fulfil this office.
So far as the priest or the prophet looks upon all
the ability he possesses as a gift, the object of which
is determined by the character of the giver, and
the nature of *His* work, so far he is a true priest
and true prophet; assuming his ability as his property, as his title, he becomes a false priest, a
false prophet; in the language of Scripture a wolf,
and not a shepherd, a destroyer of men, not their
deliverer.

But the Buddhist's conception of the Lama
supplies us with the most perfect illustration of
the difference I am endeavouring to point out.
In him is gathered up that spirit of humanity
which the Buddhist worships, and from which
he deduces his divinity. The Christian affirms
that He in whom the priesthood of the universe
rests is the eternal Son of God, that He took
human nature, united it to God, endued it with
that Spirit which dwelt without measure in Himself. He, they declare, is the Head of many
members, through each of which, so long as it

abides in Him, the same life-blood is transmitted.
The former notion, grounded upon a true and
deep feeling that there must be a centre, or that
there can be no fellowship, assumes the centre
anywhere, in a child or old man, and demands
implicit faith that in him all intelligence rests.
The other, starting from the fact that humanity
has a centre above itself, declares how He who
claimed to be this centre, in poverty, weakness,
contempt made good his title, by proving that
He could deliver the spirit of man out of its fet-
ters, that in owning Him to be its Lord it attained the freedom it was sighing for. The one
notion glorifying the intellect and spirit of man,
insists upon their doing homage to the meanest
object which they create for themselves to worship ;
the other, humbling the intellect and spirit of man
before one who they feel and confess to be their
master, offers them an expansion and exaltation
of which the knowledge and love of an absolute
and perfect Being are the only limits.

In one word, the society of the Buddhist has
no bond except the existence of something mysterious *in* the creatures who belong to it ; feeling this
to be insufficient, he invents an external supremacy,
and endues it with attributes which he knows it
does not possess ; he makes a lie, and the lie avails
him nothing, for the 300 millions which own it
compose only a mass of atoms without any principle
of cohesion, though ever seeking one. The Christian Ecclesia confesses by its very name that its

existence has its ground in the call of an Almighty
Being; that it stands only by His will; that it
is distinguished from the world to be a witness of
that true glory which man possesses when he look
upward, not downwards, to a Master, not to himself;
that, having such a call and being such a witness, it
is baptized with a Spirit of power, and truth, and
love, that it may bring all men into the divine fellowship, from which no people, or tongue, or kindred, no creature bearing the nature which Christ
redeemed from death and sin, can, except by an
act of self-will, be excluded.

I might perhaps leave the comparison here drawn
to work its way upon the consciences and hearts of
all who love truth and freedom and their kind, in
deed more than in word. But the subject is so
transcendently important at this time, that I must
present it still in one or two other lights. The
first is this. Buddhism, you see necessarily excludes
Mahometanism and Hindooism. It is the direct
contradiction of the former; Mahometanism basing
the universe upon the distinctness and absoluteness
of God. Its antipathy to the second is the great
fact of its history, the explanation of its existence.
It denies the reality of that distinction which is
involved in the doctrine of the twice-born man, as
opposed to the ordinary man. And now we find
it cannot sustain those pretensions to spirituality, on
account of which it is at war with the unspiritual
Mahometan, or that pretension to humanity and
freedom from priestcraft, on account of which it is at

war with the exclusive Brahmin. It sets their ideas
at nought; it utterly fails in realizing its own.
But we have been led to think that ideas which
have exercised such a sway over multitudes of
human beings from generation to generation, must
be realized in some way. Our philosophers have
taught us to pay this homage to the ideas of
our fellow-men; we bless them for the lesson; we
are ashamed of not having learnt it sooner, of
not having rather imparted it to them. I beseech
you seriously to ponder this question. How *may*
these ideas be realized? How may they be reconciled? And if you should, after much thinking,
find that this ancient Revelation which you were
going to cast aside as one of the false and worn-out
systems of the world, supplies that realization and
reconciliation—supplies them because it is a revelation,—on that ground, and no other—then be
sure that if you do cast it aside, or wish to prove it
something else than a revelation, the reason is not
that you care for what is expansive and comprehensive, that you hate what is formal and narrow;
this is not any longer the ground of your opposition.
Will you then with great earnestness ask yourselves, what it is?

Perhaps, however, we have been speaking only
of a verbal reconciliation; you want one which shall
be practical; one which may bear to be tried on a
great scale. Let us see then whether the case of
China, a country which you will allow to be
practical at least in its aim, to offer quite sufficient

room for a large experiment, may not supply what
you require.   If you did hear of a people which had
had for ages the strongest conviction that the
authority of the Father was the one foundation of
society, but had never been able to connect this conviction with the acknowledgement of anything mysterious and divine ; of a society which for ages had not
been able to prevent a certain body of its subjects
from dreaming that there is a mysterious and divine
word or reason speaking to the wise man, out of
which dream, however, no fruits had proceeded, but
impostures and delusions ; if you were told, that into
the heart of this society Buddhism had come, with
its strange testimony of a spirit or intellect in the
human race, the ordinary manifestations of which
are seen in very ignorant priests, its perfect manifestation often in an infant ; if you heard that these
doctrines had never been able to combine, and yet
that no one could succeed in banishing the other from
an empire in which order and unity are prized as the
highest blessings of all, nay, that experience had
proved to reluctant sages, that none of these elements
of discord could safely be extinguished, that each was
in some strange way needful to the permanence of that
which it seemed to undermine :—and if after this
you heard of a faith which assumed that the ground
of all things and all men is a Father ; that He has
spoken and does speak by his Filial Word to the
hearts and spirits of men, so making them wise,
and separating them from what is base and vain ;
that this Filial Word has been made flesh and

dwelt among men, and has given them power to become sons of God, and that through Him a Spirit is
given to dwell with men, to raise up a new spirit in
them, to unite them to each other, to make them
living portions of a living body; that men are
actually admitted by a simple rite into a Name
expressive of their adoption by the Father, separation by the Word, their inspiration by the Spirit;
that in this Name stood a universal fellowship,
which upheld the authority of earthly fathers upon
the ground of the divine relation, asserted the distinction of wise and foolish, good and evil men,
upon the ground of their following or disobeying
the monitions of that filial teacher, from whom
all right human instructors sought the power
whereby they were able to make good and useful
scholars, maintained the intercourse and communion of human beings upon the ground of their
obedience to the Spirit of order and harmony;—if,
I say, these two sets of facts were presented to you
side by side, would not you feel there was some
strange adaptation in the one to the other; that
there was in the last the secret principle and power
for which it was evident from the former that China
had through centuries been asking in vain?

But why do I speak thus? does it not sound like
the idlest of all visions to talk of our converting
Buddhists, when judging from various indications,
they are far more likely to convert us? I have
not disguised from you the Buddhist side of
Christianity; I have rejoiced to set it forth, as I

rejoiced to set forth the Mahometan and Hindoo
side of it. But, as we saw that either of these
elements might in any age become the predominant, almost the exclusive one, it is needful that
we should consider well how this third doctrine
may have in former days, may now in our own,
extinguish every other. Assuredly, there are very
distinct traces of prevalent triumphant Buddhism
in the Christian Church of periods gone by. The
history of Orders rising up first to reform society,
to rebuke organized priesthoods for their self-
indulgence, coldness, exclusiveness, to assert the
rights of the poor, to maintain that every member of Christ's flock has a calling to benefit
the rest; beginning thus nobly, and then sinking
into more intolerable despots than those against
whom they protested, self-exalted in their gifts,
their knowledge, their ignorance, or their poverty;
deceiving, and being deceived ; drawing all reverence
to their own persons on the score of their humility,
holding down the poor in slavery, whom they came
to deliver; this history contains one class of
such phenomena. In the history of Mysticism and
Quietism, telling how men have begun to seek
God with deep, earnest hearts, to denounce the
sensual, idolatrous notions others had formed of
Him, to retire into the secret chamber that there
might be no hinderance from outward things to
the clearness of the vision, to mortify their flesh,
that it might not stand in their way, have gone
on till their hearts grew puffed up and proud;

till they began to boast of wonderful discoveries vouchsafed to them alone; till they became the subjects of all nervous impressions, fantasies, disorders, as sensual as those whom they ever charged with being so; until at last they gazed on vacancy, and felt, if they had not honesty to say, 'The vision is gone, we see nothing:' here we find Christian Buddhism in another manifestation. And the lessons which these two records supply are not obsolete; either of these temptations may assault any of us again; in some form is perhaps assaulting all of us.

But chiefly should we be careful to note what common principle it was which in each of these cases turned so much seeming truth into a curse; for it is of that we have need to beware in whatever dress it may come, or if our especial work should be to encounter it in its nakedness. Unquestionably the member of the order and the solitary mystic alike yielded to the feeling, 'It is this power in me, this faculty of government, this faculty of vision, which is the great thing of all. How glorious to belong to this great society, for which I am ready to live and die; how glorious to have this capacity of conversing with the Infinite, for the sake of which I have cheerfully resigned all things!' Who could think that the deadliest poison was lurking in such words as these; that there could be the essence of all pride in such self-sacrifice? But what if men should say boldly, 'It is this power in me which is really the great power of all; it is this eye in me which creates the object it seems to behold. I will acknowledge nothing else, worship nothing else. What if this should be the language which men lisped a few years ago, and now begin to speak distinctly? Then surely there will gradually appear most of the other signs which we have traced in Buddhism, and many which could not appear in it, or in any other heathen system. First, the formation of an intellectual priesthood more utterly without the sense of a vocation, more simply glorying in its powers, therefore more intolerant, exclusive, oppressive, than any other with which this earth has ever been cursed. Next, the consciousness in that exclusive priesthood of an utter want of sympathy with actual men, notwithstanding their boast of humanity in the abstract; therefore an attempt to supply this want, as it always has been supplied, by devices to meet the taste of the vulgar, by prodigies, portents, sorceries; mysteries of science being called in as a compensation for the absence of the divine mysteries, and science being degraded into an instrument of all imposture. Finally, intellectual worship after giving birth to all forms of empiricism, ending at last in the elevation of some merely brute power to the throne of the universe; a power which will prove by his triumph, that if intellect, freedom, humanity, have no better protectors than themselves, they must be trampled down; will prove, as we are well assured, by his ultimate discomfiture, that they have another Protector, Him from whom all good and perfect gifts have come.

But it will avail little to call up such visions as these, however certain we may feel, from the testimony of history, that they will one day shew themselves to be realities, if they lead us only to the denunciation of others, to a dread of the words which *they* speak, or of the acts which *they* do.   Oftentimes I fear such denunciations and such dread conceal a very shallow faith in ourselves; oftentimes they indicate that we are sadly beset with that pride in our own intellectual powers which we attribute to others. It is ourselves we need to suspect; it is our own half conscious belief in the truths of which we talk most loudly, our own readiness to substitute the conclusions of our understandings for the divine teaching, which we ought to confess and to repent of. If we do so heartily, we shall not speak less of the operations of the divine Spirit, because some seem to contemplate them exclusively; we shall not be betrayed into the vulgar and deceitful policy of underrating the reason and faculties of men, because some seem to overvalue them; we shall not fancy that we show great dexterity and piety when we force a feeling in one direction, because its natural growth seems to be in another.

Rather, we shall regard all the tendencies of particular periods with reverence as indications of God's will, however perverted by man's ignorance and selfishness.   When we meet with a fanatical exaltation of spiritual emotions, excitements, extacies, we shall be most anxious to assert the reality of spiritual communications, not for one time, but for all; to

place them on their deepest ground, to shew how
utterly dreary man's condition would be without
them.   When we see a fanatical exaltation of human faculties and organs, then most shall we be
eager to assert their worth and sacredness; to
vindicate them from all aspersions grounded upon
the confusions incident to their imperfect exercise,
to show that they belong to every human creature
and that they cannot have too noble a cultivation.
And that both these truths may be vindicated
we shall bring them into fellowship.   The communication of the divine Spirit we shall believe
to be the only means whereby the Reason, the
Heart, the understanding, are enabled to perform their rightful functions to be vigorous, calm,
pure, in harmony with the mind of the Creator,
and with all that is truly human.   Holding all
power as a trust, every office as a stewardship, believing that the divine Spirit itself who dwells with
us is the greatest trust, the most awful stewardship
of all, we shall feel more the glory of our race
because we feel more our own insignificance; shall
be more really men, because we walk more humbly
with our God.

LECTURE VIII.

In former Lectures I have considered the relation
in which Christianity stands to the existing religious systems of the world, to Mahometanism,
Hindooism, Buddhism. In this, the last Lecture
of the course, I ought, according to the plan which
I laid down for myself, to consider in what relation
it stands to those which I called the defunct systems of ancient Persia, Egypt, Greece, Rome, and
the Gothic world. But it will strike you at once
that this subject has, in a great measure, been
anticipated.

I could not allude to the facts which justified
my use of the word defunct, in reference to these
religions, without indicating the kind of influence
which Christianity had exercised over them. I
was obliged to tell you that the worship of the
god of Light in Greece, the state religion of Rome,
the worship of Odin amongst the Goths, had given
way before the preaching of the Crucified Son of
God. I could not omit to notice the way in which
the Gospel had established itself in the Greek
cities of Egypt, or the influence it had received
from the culture previously existing in them, or
the resistance it had met with in the country dis-
tricts where the old Egyptian doctrine had its

strongest hold. I could not but speak of the revival of the old Persian faith, which took place
in the second century of the Christian era, of the
obstruction which that faith offered to the Gospel,
of its remarkable reaction upon some of the teachers
of the Gospel. I should have no excuse for tra-
velling again over this ground, though the observation we took of it was so rapid and superficial,
were it not that the facts to which I have just
alluded, taken in connexion with those which have
engaged our attention elsewhere, suggest a painful
doubt to the mind, one closely related to those
which it has been the object of the whole course
to examine.

The aspect of Christianity in the first ages,
notwithstanding the exceptions which I have noticed, is that of a youthful, growing, victorious
doctrine; its roots laid in the deepest humiliation,
its branches spreading over the earth, and reaching
to heaven. But then came Mahometanism, utterly
exterminating that Persian doctrine with which
the Christian teachers had so unsuccessfully fought,
bringing Egypt, great part of Asia, and a section
of Europe, under its yoke. When we studied the
history of this faith, we learnt that it had conquered much from the Gospel, and had scarcely,
through twelve centuries, yielded to any permanent
impression from it. The latter assertion is almost
as true of Hindooism, in spite of the establishment
of a Christian empire in the East. Buddhism still
holds a third of the globe in almost undisturbed

possession. Now a person comparing these two sets of facts will be very likely to say, " Supposing your answers to the philosophical objectors, who maintain that Christianity is a decaying, nearly obsolete, creed be ever so relevant and strong, yet what are they when weighed against this startling confirmation of their statements? Must not that faith have had a fitness for other ages, an unfitness for ours, which, during six centuries, accomplished so much, which now seems to be accomplishing almost nothing; which could then encounter the wisdom and power of those nations which we still recognize as having been the wisest and mightiest in the world, which now fails in a conflict with the ignorant and incoherent worshippers of Buddha. And if you escape by pleading that the human professors of this doctrine are less sincere and energetic than they were, what is this but saying that it depends on human energy; that it is, in fact, a human system, strong whilst those who hold it are strong—sure to wither when their zeal withers?" Such an objection as this cannot be evaded. In considering it, I shall be led to examine the different steps we have taken, beginning with the question, How did Christianity address itself to the systems with which, in its infancy, it came into collision ?

I am forced to use the word *Christianity*; for many purposes it is a convenient one. But I must remind you, that it was not a word which was familiar to the Apostles, or to those who succeeded

them in the first ages. We are not told that
they went forth preaching Christianity. The writer
of the Acts of the Apostles says that they preached
the "Kingdom of God," or "the Gospel of God,
or Christ," or "the Gospel of Christ." To expound
these words fully, would be to expound the New
Testament. But this meaning lies upon the surface of them: the Apostles came witnessing of
a Lord and King; the King and Lord of men.
The proclamation of the Crucified Man, as the
Son of God, was their Gospel, or good tidings. In
that character men were invited to receive Him.
The Apostles believed their own words; they could
therefore trust God to prove them true. If this
Man were the King of the World, strange and
ridiculous as the proposition might sound in the
ears of Jews or Heathens, He would be shewn to
be such by one means or other. Some of the Apostles knew nothing of the previous feelings and
discipline of the nations; some, as the Apostle
Paul, might have meditated on that subject, and
have conversed much with men of different opinions.
But all alike met the people among whom they
came, not with arguments to prove this true, or
that false, but with the announcement of a Person
who had a right to men's obedience, and whom
it was good that they should obey.

I. St. Paul at Athens encountered Epicureans
and Stoics; he disputed with them in the market-
place: when we are made acquainted with his
words, we find they were of this kind, "Whom

ye ignorantly worship, Him declare I unto you."
' Your poets have said, that we are the offspring
of God ; it is true ; therefore do not make Him
after the likeness of things you see and hear. He
is not far from any of us, for in Him we live,
and move, and have our being. He has appointed
a day in the which He will judge the world by
that Man whom he hath ordained ; whereof He
hath given assurance unto all men, in that He
hath raised Him from the dead.' This language,
you see, assumed that the Athenians were in search
of God ; that they were ignorantly worshipping
Him ; that they had a sense of His being a father;
that they wanted some one living, human image
of Him, to supplant those images of Him which
they had made for themselves. In Athens itself
the words were little heeded; men there were
busy seeking for some new thing to talk of; they
were occupied with schemes of the universe ; of
realities they had lost the perception. But the
teaching was adapted to all that was sound and
true in the Greek mind ; it met whatever actual
wants were awake in that mind. The Greek asked
for one who should exhibit humanity in its glory;
he was told of a Son of Man. He felt that whoever
did so exhibit it must be divine. The Son of Man
was declared to be the Son of God. He had
dreamed of one from whom the most perfect glory
man could conceive must have proceeded. He
was told of a Father. He had thought of a divine
Presence in every tree and flower. He heard of

15—2

a Presence nearer still to himself. He was not
told that he must cease to believe in powers
ruling in the Sun or Moon, or over any portion
of the earth. The Apostles had no commission
to declare there might not be such Powers, or
whether they had actual personality; they were
not to deny the existence of kingly men upon the
earth, or of angels or saints in the unseen world;
only they were to say, This is the King of kings,
the God of gods. Of his fulness must all they
have received who are anything, or ever were anything, here or elsewhere; their graces can only
be a reflection from His grace. They were to say,
He is nearer to you—more directly related to you
than all these can be; for He has taken the nature of all, and borne the sorrows and sins of all:
in Him there is nothing partial, nothing imperfect; no feebleness of sympathy in any single
direction. They were to say farther, If in any of
the objects of your reverence there is anything
earthly, sensual, evil; anything belonging to human nature in its corruption: then that must be
contrary to Him; that must be at war with Him.
So far as any creature is endued with such qualities,
it is an evil creature; it has the evil spirit; it is
not to be worshipped as if it were glorious, but
renounced as devilish; as that which would draw
you from the true estate into which Christ, by
taking your nature, has redeemed you. Therefore
the Greek mythology was met at all points by this
Gospel. What was actually or possibly good in it,

the Revelation of Christ comprehended ; what was evil and degraded it wrestled with, by proclaiming the good which it had counterfeited. But this was its charm. The Greek had a world without a centre; the preachers of the Gospel made the centre known to him. What could revolve about it, fell into its proper orbit; what determined to move independently of the centre, was seen to be unnatural and distracted.

II. How the Gospel found its way into the Egyptian heart we are not informed so distinctly. This however we may remember; Our Lord spoke to his disciples in parables ; through them he declared the mysteries of the kingdom. The facts of outward nature, the ordinary transactions of man. he recognised as a sacred writing, in which God had expressed part of his meaning, a meaning which he did not will to remain hidden, but which the Son of God unfolded. That the preachers of the Christian kingdom in Egypt should think much on this method of discovering the divine treasures was inevitable. But the substance of the communication was still the same. The Egyptian was questioning all nature to tell him of the Ammon, the hidden God : the Christian answer was still, " Him declare we unto you."

III. So it fared likewise with the Roman, whose worship had really, as we saw, a different direction from that of Greek, however in various points they might intersect each other. The clear intellect, the beautiful form, were not in his mind the consti-

tuents of Kinghood or Godhead. Order, self-government, the capacity of ruling others, submission
of individual will to law, he demanded in the
chief man ; and qualities corresponding to these
alone seemed to him divine. A faith without an
organized, harmonious society, was to the Latin
a dream. After many struggles his own mighty
commonwealth had felt that it could only continue to exist under the guidance of one head ;
and that head one uniting military and religious
titles; a ruler of armies, an object of adoration.
A king, in whom was seen the perfect fulfilment
of law—the surrender of the individual Will to
the Higher Will; the entire self-sacrifice; a King
who was the centre of a society, the head of many
members, was proclaimed by the fishermen of Ga-
lilee, by the tent-maker of Tarsus. That announcement met Roman life on all its sides and aspects;
adopted its highest maxims; overreached its noblest
idea of fellowship; shewed that the true society
had for its head one altogether unlike the emperor;
one whom he must crush, or to whom he must
bow. And so, by slow degrees, the Roman state-
idolatry, like the Greek idolatry of individual
forms and persons, perished out of the world.

IV. The Goths, again, heard the same proclamation of a kingdom of God. It did not find them
watching the embers of an expiring civilization, but
full of boyish vigour and life, and rudeness, eager
to break and subdue the earth ; possessed by the
wildest dreams of powers in earth and sea wrest-

ling for victory; doing homage to a champion
of a strong hand and seeing eye, the leader of
hosts and their prophet. With much joy, though
amidst much confusion, these barbarians welcomed
the tidings of a Mighty Redeemer in whom men
could own at once their Lord and their brother.

A redemption of man, a redemption of all that
had been lost, or disorderly in creation, was equally
assumed in the preaching to Greeks, Romans,
and Goths :—It was set forth as an accomplished
fact; as laying the only right and reasonable
ground-work for human life; as that of which the
Church, by its very existence, was to bear testimony. And it was signified in the very word
Redemption, that the partakers of it were not
brought into some novel or unnatural state, but
into that for which they were created, that which
was implied in their human constitution.

V. If this was the nature of the Christian
proclamation and its success, we may understand
where it was likely to encounter the greatest ob-
structions. The Persians believed in two rulers
of the world, one good, one evil. The great Reformer had indeed affirmed strongly that the Lord
of Light would prevail at last. He seems to have
continually hovered about the conviction that the
Prince of Darkness was a rebel against him; not
originally a divider of his throne. But he never
quite realized this conviction : he could not entirely
deny the outward universe to Ahriman ; the Persians generally believed him to be the creator of it.

The two powers were regarded as having each a right
over man, his flesh and his external circumstances
being especially the property of the dark Spirit.
What mighty evidences there seemed to be in
favour of this hypothesis! How all history, from
its beginning onwards, seemed to vouch for it! What
obstinacy in the old forms of evil; what new floods
of it were continually pouring in as from a pe-
rennial source! In the second or third centuries,
when the Roman empire was tottering to its fall,
under the weight of its own wickedness, the proofs
of Ahriman's sovereignty were surely not less
than they had been before. Had the Gospel of
Christ permanently altered this state of things?
When the Persian conversed with Christians, he
found them more ready than others to acknowledge
an evil in themselves, more sensitive to its existence
in the world. They even seemed to admit its
supremacy, and to speak of the higher and purer
state which they said Christ had established as
a deliverance out of the natural human condition;
of His saints as rebelling against the Prince of
this World. Such language, often carelessly and
ignorantly used, often misunderstood when it was
rightly used, may at first have led the Magian
to think that the Gospel had not undermined his
primitive doctrine—had rather brought new facts
in confirmation of it. And yet he will have found
Christians ready to live and die for the assertion
that Christ was the one only Lord, that all things in
heaven and earth and under the earth were subject

to Him; that no power of evil could measure itself against Him; that He held an undoubted, undivided authority. He will therefore have felt that, in spite of seeming coincidences, this faith was one with which his could not consist; that he was bound to exterminate the believers in Jesus, if he could not convert them.

We have good evidence that no question was so profoundly agitating to men's minds in the first ages as this. The Magians, as I said, succeeded in re-establishing their old doctrine, and with it the old Persian empire. But the belief in rival powers of good and evil, to the latter of which the origin of all visible things might be ascribed, spread far beyond its limits. It incorporated itself with all the religious and philosophical views of the age; it penetrated deeply into the Church of Christ, was the great characteristic of its most prevalent heresy, and mingled, in different forms and measures, with every other. Of all tests of the reality of Christian humility and faith, the greatest seems to have been the power of practically meeting this temptation, of resisting the conclusion that a perfectly good being could not be the author and ruler of the universe; that man could not really be a holy and redeemed creature; that the material world, at all events, must be given up as an evil thing. Only the simple, child-like trust which said, ' There are many things I cannot explain, but *this* I know, that the Son of God has taken my nature, and made it holy, has walked this earth

and made it holy, that he has adopted us into
fellowship with Him, and taught us to look upon
ourselves as holy, in spite of all the evil that is
in us; and to treat every creature as holy, though
corruption and death may have set their mark
upon it'—only a faith of this kind, surmounting
present appearances, and laying hold of a higher
truth, waiting calmly for them and it to be reconciled in God's good time, and meanwhile bracing
their hearts to those daily duties, which, on the
other hypothesis, would have been thrown aside
as useless and hopeless, could have hindered any
Christian from becoming inwardly, if not professedly, a Manichean. St. Augustine has given
us, in his own biography, a clear and wonderful
picture of this conflict. With a Christian mother
and a heathen father, brought up in the feeble
rhetoric of his time, but full of earnest thoughts,
which made him long to understand the nature
of himself and of God ; full, at the same time,
of violent passions seeking for gratification ; he
eagerly embraced the doctrine of the Manichean
teachers, for it served at once to explain the problem of the universe, and to justify the indul-
gences which something within him condemned.
He shews us how he was forced from speculations
upon things without, to a more awful study of that
which was passing in himself; how he learnt to
perceive that the evil within him was the resistance
of his will to a perfect and Holy Will; how this
discovery did much more than scatter his old no-

tions; how it led him to ask what that pure and
Holy Being had been doing on behalf of his race;
and whether He had offered men the means of
knowing Him and being like Him. Then the
meaning of Christ's coming dawned upon him; he
believed that the Perfect and Holy Being was
manifested in Him; that in Him man might behold his own true and proper state, and rise to
it; that in His strength we may cast off evil
from us, as an enemy which has no proper right
or dominion over us, or over any creature; that
man degrades himself when he becomes the slave
of outward things, not because they are evil in
themselves, but because they take him out of his
true condition. These truths slowly working themselves out in his mind, amidst great discourage-
ments and bitter sorrows, were those which he was
appointed to proclaim in the world, and which,
under one aspect or other, he was asserting all
his life through. Shadows of his old system were
probably often darkening his intellect; when he
was tempted to make Christianity a system, they
were nearly sure to re-appear. In general, however,
no one saw with so much clearness that evil is not
a part of the order of the universe, but essentially
disorder; that every creature seeking to dwell in
selfish independence, of necessity embraces that
disorder, and becomes a part of it; that every creature entering into God's covenant and yielding itself
to Him, becomes orderly, reasonable, blessed.

But it required more than the teaching of any

man, however wise, to check a belief which was so
natural and so plausible as this. Though only open
heretics declared that the world was essentially an
evil thing, and originated in an evil being, from
whom Christ came to deliver his disciples, and
though these statements were generally felt to be
blasphemous, yet numbers acted as if they were
true. Those who decided to live pure and holy
lives, left the world that they might do so. The
sphere of human action was more and more regarded
as an ungodly one, and those who moved in it
and ruled it, showed by their actions that they
adopted the opinion. There was no distinct, au-
dible voice, declaring, "The kingdoms of this world
are the kingdoms of our God and His Christ."
The belief silently gained ground, that there was
not a warrant for any such assertion, that the redemption which our Lord had wrought, whatever
it might mean, did not mean this.

VI. But soon a voice was heard, speaking these
words most clearly in the ears both of Persians
and Christians: "This earth is the possession of
the One Lord, the God of Abraham; He claimed
it as His when He called out Abraham, and promised that he and his seed should possess a portion
of it. The earth is still His. Those who say he
has an equal or rival are liars." This was Mahomet's language. His sword was ready to make it
good. The Magian faith, the Persian empire, fell
to pieces before it. Of all the Mahometan enterprizes this was the most startling, and that by

which its other triumphs may be best understood.
We complain of its hard outward character; the
materialism of its acts and its rewards.   But see
how well suited it was in this very respect to meet
and confute precisely the evil tendency to which
men's minds had yielded.   The denial of God's dominion over the actual world; the notion, that
though He might have some dominion somewhere
else, it was not here; this was the unbelief which
was destroying all ordinary morality, all simple trust
in a Father, was introducing atheism, or else devil-
worship among those who pretended to worship
the Holy God, and utterly to renounce evil.   Now
no mere spiritualism, if it had been ever so fine
and true, could have broken this spell.   Palpable
proofs were wanted that the kingdoms of this very
world were subject to an Unseen and Absolute
Sovereign.   And the Mahometan conquests from
generation to generation remain a testimony, not
against the Gospel, however mighty a testimony
against Christians, but for it; a testimony to one
necessary, forgotten portion of it; a proof that, if
the Church of Christ forgets its own proper position, God can raise up the strangest instruments
to do his work.

I say one portion of this Gospel; for you will
remind me that if Mahometanism asserted half the
doctrine of the text I quoted just now, " The kingdoms of this earth are God's ; " it denied the latter
half of it, " and His Christ's."   But this remark
requires to be explained and qualified by two others.

Mahometanism does, indeed, deny the fact on which
our Gospel rests, that a man is verily, and indeed,
one with the Lord of All; how that denial has
affected the whole system, I have considered in a
former Lecture. But if we remember what the
doctrine was which Mahometanism subverted, we
shall see that it involved a much greater and more
direct denial of Christ, of his rule over this
universe, and of his relation to God. The disposition to look upon the world as the possession of
an evil power, which belonged to the Persian, and to
the Christian who had caught his temper, made it
impossible even to think of it as connected with
Christ. The idea of Christ as a deliverer of man
from the power of his Creator, went far deeper
than the denial of His essential oneness with the
Creator. So far as Mahometanism helped to clear
the air of these pollutions, it removed the greatest
of all impediments to the recognition of that doctrine which it set at nought. But secondly, in
order to understand the effect of a system, and the
place it occupies in the scheme of Providence, we
should think not only of itself, but also of that
which has been called out in opposition to it. The
formation of society in modern Europe stands in
close relation to the history of Mahometanism. The
Christian nations were brought to feel that they
were connected with each other, and *what* connected them, by seeing such large portions of the
world knit together in the acknowledgement of the
Arabian prophet. Then was the feeling distinctly

realized, that all government has a Divine basis, that kings must be anointed with oil in the name of Christ, that the different members of the community hold their possessions, offices, powers, ultimately of Him ; that they depend in different gradations upon each other ; that fealty is due to that which is unseen, reverence to that which is weak. Thus, in short, those institutions, forms, habits of thought established themselves which characterize the middle ages; which may be mischievous when they exclude other principles, more clearly perceived in later times; which have become mixed with corruptions, counterfeits, and tyrannies, and confounded with them; but which are essential elements of our social existence at this day, and cannot perish until we perish. Now these embodied the other half of the great truth which St. John's words express: " The kingdoms of this world are the kingdoms of his Christ." Nor should it be forgotten, that while the Mahometan doctrine has been proved by the evidence of history to be maimed and self-destructive, so long as it stands alone, rejecting the principle of European society ; that society was continually in danger of losing its own foundation and stability, and of becoming utterly idolatrous and depraved through forgetfulness of the principle which the Mahometans put forth. The worship of the men who uttered, of the visible symbols which shadowed forth, divine truths, might have effaced those truths, but for the testimony which Islamism was permitted to bear on behalf of them.

VII.   But though the Gospel, as it was preached by the Apostles and others who followed them,
involved the assertion that the earth was redeemed
and claimed as God's possession by Christ, I am
far from affirming that this was its only or its
most characteristic affirmation.   The Old Testament was especially the witness for God's government of the *earth*.   The New speaks of the *kingdom of heaven*.   John the Baptist said the kingdom of heaven was at hand.   Our Lord illustrated
its principle in every discourse and every miracle;
His Apostles invited men to enter into it; in their
Epistles they unfolded its nature to those who had
believed the message and sought the privilege.
This kingdom they described as one of righteousness, peace and joy; the eye could not see it, but
it was most real.   It was a kingdom for the heart
and spirit of man, for that which was most properly
himself, for that in which dwell all his capacities
of sorrow, of sympathy, of trust, of hope, of love.
It was called the kingdom of God because communion with Him is the great blessedness of it.
And it is the kingdom of God because men are
brought into it that they may see themselves, their
fellow-creatures, the whole universe, as He sees
them; not partially, or merely in reference to themselves, as we naturally do.   Into this kingdom, our
Lord said, men were pressing. Experience of sorrow,
a sense of weariness and dissatisfaction with all that
was visible, the feeling of a good almost within
reach, and yet never quite attained ; above all, the

bitter consciousness of something wrong within, which needed to be purged away, of a hollow which needed to be filled up ; these were intimations to men of an unseen treasure which they were meant to possess, which only some one mightier than they could enable them to possess. Such thoughts and longings would especially haunt the hearts of poor and suffering people ; they would be rarer in men who had outward ease and comfort. But our Lord spoke of a divine power which could awaken in men the desire and capacity for this good ; of a birth from above by which their spirits might be made fit for the Kingdom of Heaven ; of an inward eye which might be opened to see it. The Apostles, when they baptized men into the Name of the Father, and of the Son, and of the Holy Ghost, bade them understand that this power was given them, and that though their bodies dwelt in Corinth or Ephesus, their real home was with Him whom they could love but not see. These were the words which stirred the hearts of the early Christians and led them to that indifference for outward things, which afterward blended so easily with the Persian notion that they were to be despised and regarded as in themselves evil. But the truth was not the less mighty because it was capable of a grievous perversion. The belief in it was the strength in which the Christian confessor lived and died. The invisible world was his dwelling ; each day he sought to become more familiar with it, to have every thought and

feeling brought into harmony with it; to show forth
more of the temper and spirit of it in his converse
with his fellow-creatures. While, indeed, he kept
his Lord's words and example in recollection, he
could not scorn any earthly task, he must look upon
all the creatures of God as good; while he remembered for what end Christ had come upon earth, he
must deem fellowship with men more blessed than
separation from them. Still it was the first gift of
his redemption, that he could rise out of this circle
of things. And when he saw to what coldness
and hardness of heart, to what gross superstitions,
men yielded, whose thoughts and aspirations were
bounded by what they could see and handle, he
could understand those words of St. Paul in which
he blessed God for having delivered the Galatians
out of this present evil world. It was an evil world,
because men made it so, by renouncing the privilege
of men; by living as if they had only senses and
were not spiritual beings capable of spiritual enjoy-
ments; as if each man could only realize the little
portion of the goods of earth which he calls his
property, and might not enter upon that inheritance
of true blessedness which all may share together, as
all may share the light of the sun together.

Now if men could so pervert these truths as
to forget that the outward world was redeemed to
be a part of God's kingdom, and if their inward life
suffered terribly from the forgetfulness, it became
manifest in the course of ages that they could quite
as easily lose sight of that which was specially and

emphatically the Christian doctrine while they seemed to admit and value its material results. Since the active energies of men's minds have been awakened, since we have felt that it is our vocation to subdue the earth, to trade, colonize and conquer, this has become the characteristic temptation of all Christian nations, perhaps I may say, especially the characteristic one of our own ; for it lies close to some of our highest virtues, our business-like habits, our preference of action to speculation, our impatience of what does not look real and practical.

Englishmen in the last century seem almost to have persuaded themselves that man is not in any sense a mysterious being, that the Gospel does not address him as such, that its main use is to make servants respectful to their masters, to keep the humble classes from interfering with the privileges of their superiors, that the kingdom of heaven is a place where certain rewards are bestowed hereafter for decency of conduct here. And those who did not act upon these maxims, but earnestly devoted themselves to a spiritual life, fancied, not unnaturally, that the desires of which they were conscious did not properly belong to human beings; that all men ought to have them, but that in fact scarcely any had them ; that the unseen world is for the select few, not for mankind.

But to Englishmen in the 18th century, the continent of India revealed itself with its treasures and its wonders. Its material treasures might help

16—2

to strengthen the worldly appetite which went in
search of them; but its wonders, if they were
well considered, might surely have supplied the
counteraction, might have proved that men everywhere need a kingdom of heaven as well as a
kingdom on earth. The Hindoo lives in a world of
thought. He is certain that divine knowledge, the
knowledge of Brahm, is the highest end of life.
He cannot be satisfied till he is united with the
Divinity. The divine man, he says, must be a
twice born-man, must be raised out of his natural
condition, must not lose himself in communion with
outward things. Indications of this faith are forced
upon the observation of every Englishman in India;
he may explain them as he will, but he cannot deny
them. Do they not say to him just, perhaps, when
the associations of his childhood are about to be cast
off altogether—' What you used to hear from your
nurse and your mother may after all mean something. You were told that you were a twice-born
man, a member of Christ, a child of God, an in-
heritor of the kingdom of heaven. May there not be
treasures nearer to you than these Indian treasures,
treasures which are yours by the clearest title, and
yet which you have never reduced into possession?
If you could impart them to these subjects of ours,
might you not do that for them which the best legis-
lation cannot do? Will you not at least ask whether
the Hindoo is wrong in thinking that man is made
for something else than to buy and sell, to eat,
drink, and die; and whether if he is right, there

is any escape from his restless self-torture, except in the calm faith that it is our Father's good pleasure to give us that kingdom which the idolator would at the price of any anguish wring from the objects of his worship?'

Here then is a voice coming from the most opposite quarter to that whence the other was brought to us—a voice of the most different kind. Yet it comes as a witness not against but for that which we have been taught to believe, a witness not for but against our indifference to it. So that these two voices compared together, may, I think, help to answer the question we have been examining, whether Christianity be not dependent for its evidence and its success upon the faith of those who promulgate it. There cannot be a truer assertion than that this is the criterion of a human system ; there cannot be a more undoubted prophecy than that the Gospel, if it be a human system, must perish, as all systems are perishing. On the other hand, if it were anything more than this, we should expect that the weakness, heartlessness, cowardice, baseness of its advocates would themselves be in some way converted into demonstrations of its truth; that when men were holding their peace respecting it, the stones would cry out. Have we not found this to be the fact? You say that Islamism has not fallen before the Cross. No, but Islamism has become one of God's witnesses for the Cross when those who pretended to bear it had really changed it for another standard. You say that Hindooism stands undisturbed by the presence of a triumphant Christian nation. Yes, for Hindooism has been wanted to teach this nation what it is very nearly forgetting itself, very nearly forcing others to forget, that Christianity is not a dream or a lie.

I believe these conclusions must be brought home, in some way or other, to the hearts as well of those who are earnest about heathen missions as of those who are indifferent to them. For what is it that palsies all efforts of this kind; what is it that produces the contrast which we have confessed between those of our own and those of earlier days? Is it not that we have more than half subscribed to the philosophical doctrine; more than half acted as if we were engaged in propagating a system of our own? Has not the impression we have conveyed to the minds of Mahometans and pagans been something of this kind: ' These Frenchmen, Dutchmen, Spaniards, or Englishmen, acknowledge a certain teacher, to whom they attach very high titles. They wish us to acknowledge their teacher instead of those whom we in Arabia, Persia, or Hindoostan, have been accustomed to honour. In other words, they wish to make us Europeans, to bring us over to their modes and habits of thinking. I know and thank God that other impressions than this have been made by the Christian missionaries of all ages and nations upon those among whom they have gone. I know that the hearts of many of them have been so possessed with the love of Him who

died for them and for all mankind, that they could
not speak of Him as if he was *their* teacher, the
Head of their sect. By their language, by their
acts, by that higher, simpler teaching which the
Bible supplies, they must have carried home to
many a broken-hearted creature, crying for a Comforter, the assurance that there is One who has
taken the nature, not of Englishmen, Frenchmen,
Spaniards, but of Man; who has entered into man's
misery and death; has borne the sins of man;
has encountered all his enemies, and vanquished
them.

The history of Missions would be barren indeed if this were not the case. But the more we
admit the worth of such testimonies—(how great
it has been we shall not know till the great day
of Revelation)—the more convinced must we be
that the old proclamation of a divine kingdom,
the old Gospel, that the Son of God, the Deliverer
of Man, has appeared, and will be shewn hereafter to be the Lord of the Universe, is the only
effectual one; that this is as fresh to-day as it was
1800 years ago, because it is a Revelation of the
Eternal Law of the Universe, which wears not out,
which grows not old; is not, in any sense whatever,
our scheme, or theory of the Universe, but is sent
to confound, to break in pieces, our theories of the
Universe, to shew how feeble and contemptible we
and our theories are; how little we or any human
creatures want a theory; what absolute need all
creatures have of a Living God, who will reveal

to us Himself; what relation there is between us and Him; how he works in us to bring us to know His purposes, and to move in accordance with them.

VIII. That last discovery is indeed one without which the words I have just been speaking would seem only words of discouragement. To look out upon the world, and see a valley covered with the dry bones of different systems, to hear them clashing together as if they might be joined to each other, and then to be told, 'It is all in vain; there is no voice which can bid the breath enter into these bones; perhaps it might have come from Christians, but it does not; they too occupy part of this valley; their creed has become one of dry bones, very dry indeed; clashing always, never uniting'—such an announcement as this, however softened by thoughts of the past or the future, must be a very mournful one. But that third great religion of the world comes to turn the current of these thoughts, to check this despondency. We are but ill provided with a theory, say the Buddhists; we have tried many, and little fruit has come of them. But this we are assured of: you Christians may not have heard it, but there is a quickening, life-giving Spirit, which is meant for humanity; which all may possess together; which alone can bring a universe out of chaos, unity out of division. Wonderful testimony to be borne from the ends of the earth, from such a medley of strange people.

so different in their thoughts, so incoherent in
their utterances! Is not the report of it like the
sound of that rushing mighty wind, which was
heard on the day of Pentecost, not indeed itself
the promised Power, but the type and herald of
it? Does it not say that we too might have cloven
tongues to declare, in different tones and measures,
according to the different thoughts, habits, and
apprehensions of men, the same wonderful works
of God, and that these tongues might be of fire
if only the same living inspiration were realized
and obeyed by us? Does it not bid us remember
that with this Spirit of Peace and Love and a
sound mind we have been sealed; that the Name
of the Father, and the Son, and the Holy Ghost,
which was to be the blessing, the permanent blessing, of Pentecost, has been bestowed upon us; that
we hold this Spirit, not as the Buddhists dream,
by our own right, to be therefore the witness of
our independence, flowing from no source whence
it may be replenished, but as the very bond of
our dependence and childhood; as the Spirit of
adoption, whereby we are to cry, Abba, Father;
as the power whereby we can ask and receive a
new life day by day. If so, there is cause enough
for humiliation in all of us, but for despair in
none. The broken limbs of the world may yet
be united, if the broken limbs of the Church were
united first. But are these the limbs of a great
system, or of a living body? Holding the first
opinion of herself, the Church has been either held

artificially together, the children within her groaning under the bondage to which she has subjected
them, those without hearing in her invitation a
message not of deliverance but of heavier slavery;
or else, these artificial joints and fastenings being
removed, she has split into fragments, with which
those who are clinging to them become more and
more dissatisfied, which offer to those without an
excuse for adhering to the tradition of their fathers,
be it ever so dreary, till those who bid them leave
it are agreed what they should adopt in its place.
But if the Scripture language be true, if the Church
be a body constituted in a Head, the Buddhist
proclamation carries with it the reproof and consolation which we require.   There is a Power
which can bring us not into some imaginary condition of excellence, but precisely into our true
condition: can remove the individual interests,
selfish feelings, national antipathies, narrow apprehensions which all our efforts to produce unity
only evoke and strengthen, can bring down our
high notions and conceits of what we are and
what we can do, can enable us to be God's servants and to do His work in the world which
He has redeemed.   Having confessed our rebellion
against this Spirit, and sought the renewal of
it in us and in the whole Church, we shall no
longer say, as we have been tempted to say,
' The power of evil is supreme over the universe;
only there have been some special deliverances
vouchsafed to us;' we shall, from our hearts, abjure

such blasphemous Manicheism; we shall say boldly
to all people among whom we go, 'The devil is
not your master, he has no right to your worship:
the God, in whom is light and no darkness at all,
has claimed you and the whole creation for His
own. His marvellous light is as much for you
as for us. We only enjoy it upon the condition
of renouncing all exclusive claim to it, upon the
condition of bidding you enter into it.'

IX. Buddhism, then, like Hindooism and Mahometanism, has its lesson for us. We are debtors
to all these in a double sense. Nor, I think, is it
otherwise with those modern infidels whose objections I have been considering throughout this course.
Our obligations to them are not slight if they have
been sent to break down a low grovelling notion we
had formed of our own position and work; if they
have been employed to convince us that human
systems must indeed perish, one and all, that
what survives must be something of a much
higher derivation, of a more eternal character.
We owe them the deepest gratitude if they have led
us to ask ourselves more earnestly whether there is
any faith, and what kind of faith it is, which must
belong, not to races or nations, but to mankind;
still more, if they have forced us to the conclusion,
that the real test, whether there be such a faith,
and whether it has been made known to us must be
action, not argument; that if it exist, it must
shew that it exists; that if it have power, it must
put forth its power. So, in this 19th century, the

opponents of Christianity will return to the maxim
which the wisest of them announced in the first :
" If this be of men, it will come to nought ; if it be
of God, we cannot overthrow it."

I have been anxious in these Lectures to
shew that I did regard this practical experiment
of our faith as the really decisive one. In com-
pliance with the directions of Boyle, I sought
for that which seemed to be the most prevailing
form of unbelief in our day; and I found in it
the tendency to look upon all theology as having
its origin in the spiritual nature and faculties of
man.   This was assumed undoubtedly to be the
explanation of other systems, why not apply it to
Christianity? The questions we have asked have
then been, 'Is it the adequate explanation of
any system? Do not *all* demand another ground
than the human one? Is not Christianity the
consistent assertor of that higher ground? Does
it not distinctly and consistently refer every human
feeling and consciousness to that ground? Is it
not *for this reason* able to interpret and reconcile
the other religions of the earth? Does it not in
this way prove itself to be *not* a human system, but
the Revelation, which human beings require?'

'Prove!' you cry: 'Yes, on paper! It is
easy to prove many things about human creatures
when you are not actually dealing with them.'
Assuredly, most easy.   It was of this that the
other clauses of Boyle's Will warned me.   They
said very significantly, ' Your business is to urge

upon your countrymen the duty of not proving
Christianity upon paper; but of entering into actual intercourse with Jews, Mussulmans, Hindoos,
Buddhists, for the purpose of shewing that it is
a reality.' Accordingly, I have never lost sight of
this object. My questions have been, 'How may we
bring Christianity into contact with the actual convictions of these different people? How may we
put it upon the broadest trial? Where have other
instruments and appliances failed? for that is the
point to which we would apply this. Where may
it most certainly prove its inefficiency, if it be
inefficient?' In no case have I wished to dis-
guise any apparent symptoms of its failure. I
have entreated Christians and infidels to inves-
tigate these, that they may ascertain the causes of
them. And lest you should fancy, from the view
I took of these systems, that I was recommend-
ing some new method of dealing with them, which
could only be learnt and applied after a long discipline, and at last would be scarcely adapted to
simple ministers of the Gospel, I have endeavoured
to shew you in this Lecture, that precisely the course
I have suggested is that which the preachers of the
Gospel in the first ages actually adopted, that our
departures from it have arisen from want of simple
faith; that the discipline we require is especially
one to restore this faith. And lest, from what
has been just said about the unity of Christians,
you should conclude that I suppose missions to the
heathen should be deferred till some indefinite time

when the nations of Christendom can make a simultaneous assault upon the outlying world, I would remind you that my reference to the first ages, and to the successful missionary efforts of any subsequent age, precludes such a notion. What nation of the earth owes its Church to a simultaneous effort among nations or among men? If any one nation takes its stand upon its true ground as a member of that body whereof Christ is the Head, that nation becomes a witness to all Christian nations of their true Unity, if they care ever so little for it; that nation can fulfil its own task of vindicating the truths which its heathen subjects confess, by imparting to them the truths which they want, though all the other Christian nations should smile or frown upon its endeavours. Any Christian man who takes his stand upon the same ground of unity in the Church whereof Christ is the Head, who acts consistently with that position, fulfilling the office to which he is called, and not seeking some other to please himself, may become a witness in every land to which he goes of the fellowship into which his baptism has brought him; may in his words or life expound the principle of this fellowship; may shew how universal its privileges are, and how each may for himself partake of them.

But I know that there must be many on whom the often-repeated words, 'There are heathens at our doors, we ourselves are half heathens; leave Buddhists and Mahometans till you have provided for these,' will have an effect sufficient to destroy

their interest in all such exhortations. One answer
to these objections is well-known, and has been sufficiently used. If Englishmen did abstain rigidly
from all intercourse with Mahometans, Hindoos,
Buddhists, if no body of our countrymen were
engaged in trading with other countries, or in
conquering them, or in keeping possession of them,
the interdiction of all spiritual communication
might be judicious—at all events possible. But
as the points at issue are, what *kind* of communication shall we hold with these people, what *kind*
of help or protection shall we extend to them: if
they are spiritual creatures, and as such must in
some way be dealt with, then how? since this, I
say, is the fair statement of the case, such appeals
to our home sympathies seem rather capricious
and rhetorical than benevolent or sensible. But this
is not the only reply which is suggested by our
particular circumstances; or which lies in the nature
of the subject itself. A faith which boasts to be
for humanity cannot test its strength unless it is
content to deal with men in all possible conditions.
If it limit itself to England, it will adapt itself to
the habits and fashions and prejudices of England,
and of England too in a particular age. But doing
this, it never will reach the hearts of Englishmen.
You say, 'Try your Christianity upon the cotton-
spinners of Manchester, upon the hardware men of
Birmingham; if it fails with them, do you expect
it will succeed in Persia and Thibet?' But we
know it will fail, it must fail in Birmingham and

Manchester, if it address the people in those places
mainly as spinners and workers in hardware. This
has just been the mistake we have made. We have
looked upon these 'hands' as created to work for us;
we have asked for a religion which should keep the
'hands' in the state in which they will do most work
and give the least trouble. But it is found that they
are men who use these hands; and that which is a
religion for hands, is not one for men. Therefore it
becomes more evident every day that there is a
demand in Manchester and Birmingham for that
which, till we understand human beings better, we
cannot supply. To acquire that understanding we
need not grudge a journey to Persia or Thibet ; we
need not think it an idle task to inquire what the
people want, who are not called to spin cotton
or work in hardware, but who are creatures of
the same kind with those who do. When thoughtful men say that a working age of the world is
about to begin, they mean, I suppose, an age in
which those essential qualities of humanity which
belong to working men as much as to all others, shall
be more prized than the accidents by which one
class is separated from another. Most important is
it then to ascertain whether we are holding a faith
which addresses us as members of a class, a class
of fine gentlemen, philosophers, divines, or any
other ; or one which addresses us as men, which
explains the problems of our human life. Two
centuries ago Boyle was led in deep anguish of
spirit to consider that question for himself; for

himself, and not I think without something of the like anguish, must each one of us consider it in this day. We are told that circumstances have changed, that our condition is a different one from his. Doubtless, the saying is true; circumstances are always changing; but the necessities of man's being do not change. What was true of man generations ago, is true now. If our condition is different from that of men two centuries back, the difference is this : we are come nearer to the great crisis of all controversies, there is less power of hiding ourselves from realities amidst shadows and appearances. Thanks be to God that such a time has come, terrible as it may be to many, nay to all of us! For this is the time which will shew that His truth is not of man, neither by man; but that it is for man, here and everywhere. Only then when the grass withereth, and the flower fadeth,— so speaks individual experience, so speaks the voice of history—is it known assuredly that the Word of our God shall stand for ever.

THE END.

For EU product safety concerns, contact us at Calle de José Abascal, 56–1°, 28003 Madrid, Spain or eugpsr@cambridge.org.